# The Art of
# Wok Cooking

*from*

WEST BEND®

# Contents

ISBN 0-8249-0014-6
Copyright © MCMLXXXIV by Ideals Publishing Corp.
All rights reserved.
Printed and bound in the United States of America.

Published by Ideals Publishing Corporation
11315 Watertown Plank Road
Milwaukee, Wisconsin 53226
Published simultaneously in Canada

® The name West Bend and
the West Bend Logo are
Trademarks of Dart Industries, Inc.

Pork Strips with Szechwan Sauce, page 61

# Wok Basics

Cooking in a wok is not difficult; it is different. It requires a feel for split-second timing, a sense of sequence and a knowledge of the amount of heat that will produce the best results. As you stir and toss food in the wok, your eyes will be on the food but your mind will be anticipating the next step.

Stir-frying is the most-used method of wok cookery. It is fast and fun, and results in delicious-tasting food. Searing meat and vegetables at high heat seals in their flavors, nutrients and juices while at the same time preserving their textures. A wonderful form of self-expression, stir-frying in a wok is a lot like tossing a salad. With a wooden spoon in each hand, you maintain a constant motion of tossing and turning food over high heat.

Wok cookery need not necessarily mean Chinese cooking, although it is best illustrated in that ancient cuisine. Several of the recipes for basic, familiar foods in this book are not Chinese in origin. A wok can also be used in place of a conventional skillet, saucepan or fryer. It can be a steamer when fitted with a rack or bamboo basket.

Wok cookery is very adaptable. After you've made several stir-fry recipes in this book, you'll understand the technique, enabling you to combine your favorite foods in dishes which reflect your own personal style and taste preferences.

Using a wok, you can prepare nutritious, flavorful, crisp and colorful foods in a matter of minutes.

**BEFORE USING YOUR WEST BEND ELECTRIC WOK...**

Review the care and use instructions booklet packaged with your wok before using. Keep this instruction booklet with your cookbook for future reference.

**THE BASICS OF WOK COOKING**

Successful cooking in a wok depends on proper utensils and several cutting techniques and cooking methods.

# Wok Basics

## UTENSILS

**Chopsticks** Wooden sticks that taper to points. They are used for stirring ingredients, beating eggs, in addition to being eating utensils.

**Cleaver** A broad, rectangular-bladed knife used for cutting, chopping, shredding, slicing and transferring food. A large chef's knife may also be used.

**Ladle** A smooth-edged metal utensil with rounded scoop used to remove or serve food.

**Steamer** Available in two forms. One is bamboo and can be placed directly into the wok over boiling water and covered to steam or reheat foods. The second is a metal rack that fits into the lower portion of the wok over boiling water. Foods may be placed on the rack or in heatproof bowls or plates on the rack. The wok is then covered for steaming.

**Strainer** A utensil with a shallow wire-net scoop and a bamboo or wooden handle. It is used to remove foods from hot oil or liquid. A metal slotted spoon may also be used as a strainer.

**Tempura Rack** A metal rack that fits onto the top edge of the wok and drains foods after tempura frying.

**Wok** An all-purpose concave cooking pan with sloping sides that is thought to be one of the oldest cooking utensils. It is used for stir-frying, frying, braising, stewing, blanching and steaming. Its shape confines high temperatures to the base for fast cooking. Heat lessens up the sides of wok to keep foods warm.

**Wooden Spoons** Two long-handled wooden spoons, one held in each hand, for constant stirring of foods while stir-frying.

## CUTTING TECHNIQUES

All ingredients for stir-frying in a wok should be cut in thin uniform-size pieces for attractive appearance and even, fast cooking. It is easier to cut meat in thin slices if it is partially frozen; then it will not slip under the pressure of a knife. Always slice across the grain to retain tenderness. Sharp knives are a

# Wok Basics

must. Following are the cutting techniques used on most meats and vegetables:

1. **Slicing or Straight Cutting:** Hold the knife or cleaver straight up and down to cut to the desired thickness, usually from paper-thin to ½ inch thick.

2. **Shredding or Julienne Slicing:** Food is first sliced, then cut into uniform strips about the size of matchsticks. Shreds vary from ⅛ to ¼ inch thick and from 1½ to 2 inches long.

3. **Cubing:** Food is first sliced ½ inch thick, then again across the slices every ½ inch to produce ½-inch cubes.

4. **Chopping:** This is the coarsest cut and results in ½-inch pieces.

5. **Dicing:** Food is first sliced into thin slices, then into thin strips, then into small pieces varying from ¼ to ½ inch square.

6. **Mincing:** Food is chopped into rice-size pieces. It is much easier to mince vegetables if they are first chopped or diced.

7. **Diagonal Cutting:** Used mostly for vegetables. The knife or cleaver is held at a 45-degree angle for slicing. Practice with celery. Position the knife blade about ¾ inch from the end of the rib. Slant the knife blade away from you and slice the stalk with a sharp, angled cut. Discard this first irregular piece. Continue cutting at the same slant in small, regular intervals to produce thin, flat slices.

8. **Rolled or Oblique Cutting:** Used mostly for vegetables. The knife or cleaver is held at an angle to the food while the opposite hand rolls the food before the next cut is made, thus changing the angle of the cut. Practice with a carrot. Make a diagonal cut across the carrot; discard the first piece. Then, keeping the knife in the same position, roll the carrot over and cut through it diagonally again to form a piece with two slanted sides. Continue rolling and cutting in this manner.

## COOKING METHODS

A wok is a versatile cooking utensil. All of the following cooking methods are possible in a wok.

# Wok Basics

**Stir-Frying** The most common cooking method in a wok, stir-frying is the vigorous stirring of food in a small amount of oil over high cooking temperatures for brief cooking times, usually just a few minutes. Before beginning, read the recipe through. Have all ingredients cut and/or measured as directed; place in small bowls arranged in the order in which they will be added to the wok. This can be done hours in advance. Have all utensils and serving pieces at easy access. Stir-frying should be done just before serving and requires swift movements and split-second timing. Get used to the sound of sizzling, a sign of successful stir-frying. Preheat recommended amount of oil in uncovered wok at recommended cooking temperature. Then proceed as the recipe directs.

**Frying** Foods are cooked in hot oil. Always preheat recommended amount of oil in uncovered wok at recommended temperature setting.

**Blanching** Food is parboiled in boiling water. When stir-frying, this is usually done to partially cook vegetables before they are completely cooked in the wok. They are immersed in boiling water, partially cooked and rinsed in cold water to stop the cooking and to set bright color.

**Braising** Food cooks in a small amount of liquid in a covered wok at a simmering temperature.

**Steaming** This cooking method uses no oil. It can be done on a rack or in a bamboo steamer in a wok. To steam food, place the rack above 2 to 3 inches of water in the wok. The rack and food should not touch the water. Bring the water to a rapid boil, place the food on the rack or on a shallow heatproof plate on the rack. Cover the wok. If using a bamboo basket, place the food in it, cover the basket with the bamboo lid and place over boiling water. It is not necessary to cover the wok.

**Simmering** Food cooks at temperatures low enough to cause bubbles to appear and barely break the surface of the cooking liquid.

# Appetizers

## Chinese-Flavored Beef

Makes approximately 40 pieces
Preparation Time: 15 minutes; 1 hour to cook

2 tablespoons peanut oil
4 green onions, cut in 1-inch pieces
1 tablespoon peeled and minced fresh gingerroot
1 pound boneless beef chuck, cut in 1-inch cubes
Sauce Mixture

Heat oil in uncovered wok at 375°. Add onions and gingerroot; stir-fry 1 minute. Add beef cubes; stir-fry 2 to 3 minutes or until browned. Add Sauce Mixture; bring to a boil. Cover, reduce heat to "simmer" and cook 30 minutes. Uncover; increase heat to 350°; cook until sauce thickens, about 20-25 minutes. Remove from wok; serve hot with picks for spearing meat.

### Sauce Mixture

¼ cup sugar
2 tablespoons soy sauce
⅓ cup dry sherry
1 cup water
½ teaspoon dried red pepper flakes

Mix all ingredients until sugar dissolves.

## Crab Won Tons

Makes 36
Preparation Time: 30 minutes

1 8-ounce package cream cheese, softened
1 6-ounce package frozen crab meat, thawed and drained
36 won ton skins
3 cups peanut oil
Sweet and Sour Sauce (Recipe on page 43)

Mix cream cheese and crab meat in bowl. Place 1 teaspoon in middle of won ton skin; moisten edges with cold water; fold to form triangle; seal edges by pressing together. Prepare remaining won tons in same manner. Heat oil in uncovered wok at 375°. Fry won tons on both sides until golden. Drain on paper towels; keep warm. Serve with Sweet and Sour Sauce for dipping.

## Nacho Won Tons

Makes 20
Preparation Time: 20 minutes

- 6 **ounces sharp Cheddar cheese, shredded**
- 20 **won ton skins**
- 1 **4-ounce can chopped mild** or **hot green chilies, drained**
- 3 **cups peanut oil**

Dividing cheese equally, place in middle of each won ton skin. Top each with ¼ teaspoon chilies. Moisten edges of won ton skins with cold water; fold to form triangle, sealing edges. Heat oil in uncovered wok at 375°. Fry won tons on both sides until browned. Drain on paper towels. Serve immediately.

## Fried Won Tons

Makes approximately 50
Preparation Time: 30 minutes; 10 minutes to cook

- ¼ **pound ground lean pork** or **chicken** or **beef**
- 1 **6-ounce can shrimp, drained and minced**
- ¼ **cup minced mushrooms**
- ¼ **cup diced water chestnuts**
- 1 **green onion, finely chopped**
- 2 **egg yolks**
- 1 **tablespoon soy sauce**
- 1½ **teaspoons peanut oil**
- ¾ **pound won ton skins (about 50)**
- 3 **cups peanut oil**
  **Won Ton Sauce**

Mix first 8 ingredients in wok. Set heat at 325° and cook, stirring often, about 5 minutes. Cool. Clean and dry wok. Place about 1 tablespoon mixture in middle of each won ton skin. Moisten edges of wrapper with cold water; fold in half diagonally to form triangle; press edges together to seal. Fry won tons in oil heated at 375° in uncovered wok until golden on both sides; drain on paper towels. Serve with sauce.

**Note:** Can be prepared 1 hour in advance; keep warm in 200° oven.

### Won Ton Sauce

- 2 **tablespoons cornstarch**
- 3 **tablespoons light brown sugar, packed**
- ¼ **cup soy sauce**
- ¾ **cup water**
- 1 **clove garlic, peeled and sliced**
- 1 **tablespoon peanut oil**

Stir first 4 ingredients until smooth. Fry garlic in hot oil in uncovered wok at 250° until light brown. Remove garlic; set aside. Slowly pour cornstarch mixture into hot oil; cook, stirring, until thickened. Top with fried garlic.

## Egg Rolls

Makes 4 to 5 dozen
Preparation Time: 1 hour

**2 tablespoons peanut oil**
**3 ribs celery, cut in 1-inch julienne pieces**
**6 green onions, cut in 1-inch julienne pieces**
**¾ teaspoon salt**
**¾ teaspoon sugar**
**1½ pounds finely chopped lean pork or chicken or shrimp**
**1 8-ounce can sliced bamboo shoots, drained and coarsely chopped**
**2 cups fresh bean sprouts**
**2 tablespoons soy sauce**
**2 tablespoons dry sherry**
**1 1-pound package egg roll skins**
**1 egg white, lightly beaten**
**3 cups peanut oil**
**Sweet and Sour Sauce (Recipe on page 43) or Hot Mustard Sauce (Recipe on page 44) or Duck Sauce**

Heat 1 tablespoon oil in uncovered wok at 375°. Add next 4 ingredients; stir-fry 2 minutes. Remove to large bowl; set aside. Heat 1½ teaspoons oil in wok until hot; add pork and bamboo shoots; stir-fry 1 minute. Remove to bowl. Heat remaining 1½ teaspoons oil in wok until hot; add bean sprouts; stir-fry 2 minutes; remove to bowl. Turn wok OFF. Clean and dry when cool. Stir soy sauce and sherry into mixture in bowl. Place in strainer to drain thoroughly, at least 10 minutes. Place 1 egg roll skin on counter with a corner toward you. Put 1 tablespoon filling in rectangular mound on center of wrapper. Fold bottom corner of wrapper up over filling; overlap 2 opposite side corners. Moisten 4th or top corner with egg white; fold over to form roll. Heat oil in uncovered wok at 375°. Fry egg rolls, two to three at a time, until golden brown. Drain on paper towels. Serve with sauce of your choice.

**Note:** After frying, egg rolls can be covered and refrigerated no longer than 24 hours. Heat, uncovered, in 350° oven about 15 minutes or until heated through.

Fried Won Tons, page 9
Egg Rolls, this page

# Appetizers

## Gingered Pork Balls

Makes 12 to 16
Preparation Time: 20 minutes

- **1 pound ground pork**
- **1 cup coarsely chopped water chestnuts**
- **½ teaspoon peeled and chopped fresh gingerroot**
- **1 egg, lightly beaten**
- **1 tablespoon soy sauce Cornstarch**
- **3 cups peanut oil**

Mix first 5 ingredients lightly. Shape into bite-size balls; roll lightly in cornstarch. Heat oil in uncovered wok at 375°. Add pork balls, a few at a time; fry until golden brown and cooked through, about 3 to 4 minutes. Drain on paper towels; serve hot with wooden picks.

## Oriental Spareribs

Makes approximately 2 dozen
Preparation Time: 1½ hours

- **2 cups water**
- **½ cup soy sauce**
- **1 clove garlic, peeled and minced**
- **3 pounds spareribs, cut in 2-inch pieces**
- **2 tablespoons packed light brown sugar**
- **1 tablespoon cornstarch**
- **1 tablespoon sesame seed**
- **2 tablespoons chopped green onion**
- **1 ¼-inch slice fresh gingerroot, peeled and minced**

Mix water, ¼ cup soy sauce and garlic in wok. Add spareribs; bring to boil at 225°. Reduce heat to "simmer"; cover, cook 1 hour. Remove cover; bring to boil at 225°; cook 20 minutes. Drain; reserve ¼ cup cooking liquid. Mix remaining ¼ cup soy sauce and remaining ingredients. Place spareribs and reserved ¼ cup cooking liquid in wok at 325°. Pour seasoned soy sauce over ribs; cook, spooning sauce over ribs until it thickens and adheres to ribs, about 10 minutes. Serve warm.

**Note:** These can be made 3 to 4 hours in advance; reheat in microwave oven or in conventional 350° oven 10 minutes.

# Appetizers

## Fried Walnuts

Makes approximately 4 cups
Preparation Time: 5 minutes; overnight to marinate; 10 to 15 minutes to cook

1 cup water
¾ cup sugar
1 pound walnut halves
1 cup peanut oil

Combine water and sugar in saucepan; cook 5 minutes to make syrup. Place walnuts in jar with cover; top with syrup. Cool; cover; let stand overnight; drain. Heat oil in uncovered wok at 325°. Add nuts in batches; fry 1 to 2 minutes. Remove from oil with strainer. Drain on paper towels. Serve immediately.

## Shrimp Toast

Makes approximately 32 pieces
Preparation Time: 20 minutes; 10 minutes to cook

1 6-ounce can shrimp, drained and minced
3 ounces ground lean pork
1½ teaspoons dry sherry
1½ teaspoons soy sauce
½ teaspoon salt
¼ teaspoon freshly ground black pepper
¼ cup finely chopped green onions
¾ teaspoon cornstarch
½ teaspoon sesame oil
2 eggs
7 to 8 slices thin white bread
⅓ cup fine dry bread crumbs
1 cup peanut oil

Mix shrimp with next 8 ingredients and 1 egg. Spread shrimp mixture generously over 1 side of each slice of bread. Beat remaining egg in bowl; brush over bread and filling. Sprinkle bread crumbs over filling. Cut bread diagonally into quarters. Heat oil in uncovered wok at 375°. Slide bread triangles, a few at a time, filling-side-down, into hot oil. Fry until golden; turn to brown other side. Drain on paper towels. Serve hot.

Note: Shrimp Toast can be made 30 minutes in advance; keep warm in 200° oven.

# Soups

## Noodles and Vegetables in Broth

Makes 6 servings
Preparation Time: 20 minutes

8 ounces wide egg noodles
6 cups chicken stock
2 cups cubed cooked chicken, turkey, pork or ham
1 carrot, pared and cut in thin diagonal slices
1 large rib celery, cut in thin diagonal slices
2 green onions, halved lengthwise and cut diagonally in 1-inch pieces
½ cup thinly sliced bok choy (Chinese cabbage)

2 tablespoons soy sauce
Salt and freshly ground white pepper to taste

Cook noodles according to package directions; drain; rinse under cold running water to stop cooking; set aside. Heat chicken stock in uncovered wok at 225°. Add next 6 ingredients; season to taste with salt and pepper. Simmer 5 to 10 minutes to just barely cook vegetables. Divide noodles among 6 soup bowls; ladle in soup. Serve immediately.

## Oriental Spring Soup

Makes 6 servings
Preparation Time: 10 minutes; 15 minutes to cook

5 cups chicken stock
½ cup julienne-cut carrot
½ cup peas, fresh or frozen
½ cup fresh spinach leaves, washed, stems discarded, shredded
¼ cup finely sliced green onion
2 tablespoons minced fresh parsley
Salt and freshly ground white pepper to taste

Bring chicken stock to simmer in uncovered wok at 225°. Add carrot and peas; cook 5 minutes. Add spinach, green onion and parsley; simmer 2 minutes. Add salt and pepper to taste. Serve immediately.

Clockwise, from top:
Won Ton Soup, page 16
Japanese Soup, page 18
Egg Drop Soup with Shrimp, page 19

# Soups

## Watercress Soup with Ham Shreds

Makes 6 to 8 servings
Preparation Time: 30 minutes

- 8 **cups chicken stock**
- ½ **teaspoon five-spice powder**
- 2 **teaspoons salt**
- 1 **teaspoon sugar**
- 2 **tablespoons dry sherry**
- 2 **¼-inch slices fresh gingerroot, peeled**
- 4 **green onions, sliced**
- 2 **bunches watercress, washed, stems discarded**
- ½ **cup thinly sliced ham**

Put first 7 ingredients in wok. Bring to boil at 225°; cook 10 minutes; strain, reserving stock. Return stock to wok; bring to boil at 225°; add watercress and ham; return to boil. Serve immediately.

## Won Ton Soup

Makes 6 servings plus leftover won tons
Preparation Time: 1 hour; 10 minutes to cook

- 6 **Chinese dried black mushrooms, soaked in hot water 20 minutes, drained, stems discarded, caps minced**
- ¼ **pound ground lean pork**
- ¼ **pound shrimp, coarsely chopped**
- 3 **teaspoons minced green onion**
- 2 **tablespoons soy sauce**
- ½ **teaspoon salt**
- 1 **teaspoon sesame oil Dash freshly ground white pepper**
- 1 **pound won ton skins**
- 1 **egg white, lightly beaten**
- 6 **cups hot chicken stock Finely sliced green onions, optional**

Mix first 8 ingredients. Place ½ teaspoon filling in center of each won ton skin. Moisten edges with egg white; fold in triangle; press edges to seal. Moisten the two far points of triangle with water; press together firmly. Makes about 55 won tons. Bring 2 quarts of water to a boil in wok at 250°. Drop 18 won tons into boiling water; cook 10 minutes; drain. Place 3 won tons in each of 6 soup bowls; fill with hot chicken stock; garnish with green onions, if desired. Serve immediately.

**Note:** Remaining won tons can be frozen. It is not necessary to thaw before cooking.

## Far East Tofu Soup

Makes 4 to 6 servings
Preparation Time: 20 minutes; 30 minutes to cook

2 tablespoons peanut oil
1½ cups sliced fresh mushrooms
3 large cloves garlic, peeled and crushed
½ teaspoon peeled and minced fresh gingerroot
3 tablespoons soy sauce
2½ cups chicken stock
1½ cups water
1 cup uncooked egg noodles
1 unpeeled medium zucchini, cut in ½-inch pieces
1 cup cleaned and finely chopped fresh spinach
¼ pound tofu, cut in ½-inch cubes
⅛ cup finely chopped green onions including tops

Heat oil in uncovered wok at 375°. Add next 3 ingredients; stir-fry 2 minutes. Add soy sauce; turn wok OFF. Bring stock and water to boil in another wok at 225° or in a large saucepan; add noodles; boil 2 minutes; reduce heat to "simmer"; add zucchini and spinach; simmer 6 to 8 minutes. Add tofu and reserved mushroom mixture; simmer 8 to 10 minutes. Garnish with green onions. Serve immediately.

## Velvet Corn Soup

Makes 6 to 8 servings
Preparation Time: 10 minutes; 15 minutes to cook

6 cups hot chicken stock
2 tablespoons cornstarch
1 tablespoon peanut oil
4 green onions, white part only, minced
2 cups cream-style corn, pureed in food processor or blender
¼ teaspoon salt
¼ teaspoon freshly ground white pepper
1 tablespoon dry sherry
2 egg whites, lightly beaten until frothy
2 tablespoons minced cooked ham

Pour ¼ cup chicken stock over corn-starch in small bowl; stir to combine; set aside. Heat oil in uncovered wok at 325°. Add onions; stir-fry 30 to 45 seconds. Add remaining stock, corn, salt, pepper and sherry; reduce heat to "simmer" for 15 minutes. Increase heat to 225°; bring soup to boil; add corn-starch mixture. Stir until soup is slightly thickened, about 3 minutes. Turn wok OFF; add egg whites; stir to combine. Stir in ham; serve immediately.

# Soups

## Japanese Soup

Makes 6 to 8 servings
Preparation Time: 25 minutes

6 cups chicken stock
¼ cup dry sherry
1½ tablespoons soy sauce
6 to 8 fresh mushrooms, wiped clean and thinly sliced
1 teaspoon lemon juice
6 green onions, cut in ½-inch diagonal slices
1 small carrot, pared and cut in thin diagonal slices
¼ pound tiny shelled shrimp, optional

Bring stock to simmer in uncovered wok at 225°. Stir in sherry and soy sauce; simmer 5 minutes. Add remaining ingredients; bring to boil; simmer 5 minutes. Serve immediately.

## Spinach Soup with Pork Balls

Makes 4 servings
Preparation Time: 1 hour

6 cups chicken stock
2 ¼-inch peeled slices fresh gingerroot
4 Chinese dried black mushrooms, soaked in hot water 20 minutes, drained, stems discarded, caps thinly sliced
Salt and freshly ground white pepper to taste
2 green onions, minced
¼ cup minced water chestnuts
½ pound lean ground pork
1 tablespoon soy sauce
1 teaspoon dry sherry
2 teaspoons cornstarch
½ cup loosely packed spinach leaves, washed, stems discarded, shredded

Bring chicken stock and 2 slices gingerroot to simmer in uncovered wok at 225°. Reduce heat to "simmer"; add mushrooms, salt and pepper; simmer 15 minutes. Remove gingerroot. Mix next 6 ingredients; form into 12 1¼-inch balls. Add pork balls to stock; cover; simmer 30 minutes or until cooked through. Add spinach 3 minutes before serving; serve immediately.

## Chinese Cucumber Soup

Makes 6 to 8 servings
Preparation Time: 30 minutes

- 1 **tablespoon dry sherry**
- 2 **tablespoons soy sauce**
- 1 **tablespoon cornstarch**
- ½ **pound boned and skinned chicken breast** or **finely shredded lean pork**
- 2 **tablespoons peanut oil**
- 6 **cups chicken stock**
- 2 **green onions, thinly sliced**
- 1 **medium cucumber, peeled, split lengthwise, seeds removed, diced**
- 1½ **teaspoons salt**
- ¼ **teaspoon freshly ground white pepper**
- 1 **egg, lightly beaten**

Mix first 3 ingredients in bowl; add chicken; stir to coat. Heat oil in uncovered wok at 350°. Add chicken; stir-fry 3 to 5 minutes. Add chicken stock; reduce heat to "simmer" for 10 to 12 minutes. Add next 4 ingredients; simmer 5 minutes. Increase heat to 250°; bring soup to fast boil; turn wok OFF; stir in egg. Serve immediately.

## Egg Drop Soup with Shrimp

Makes 6 to 8 servings
Preparation Time: 20 minutes

- 6 **cups chicken stock**
  **Salt and freshly ground white pepper to taste**
  **Pinch cayenne pepper**
- ½ **cup frozen peas**
- 16 **medium shrimp, shelled and deveined**
- 2 **tablespoons cornstarch mixed with ¼ cup cold water**
- 2 **eggs, lightly beaten with 1 teaspoon soy sauce**
- 2 **green onions, thinly sliced**

Heat chicken stock, salt, pepper and cayenne pepper in uncovered wok at 225° to just under a boil. Add peas; cook 1 minute. Add shrimp; cook until pink. Add cornstarch mixture, stirring until slightly thickened. Turn wok OFF; swirl in eggs using fork. Garnish with onions; serve immediately.

# Soups

## Hot and Sour Soup

Makes 4 to 6 servings
Preparation Time: 25 minutes; 20 minutes to cook

4 cups chicken stock
6 ounces lean pork or chicken breast, cut in julienne strips
½ cup tofu, cut in julienne strips
½ cup bamboo shoots, cut in julienne strips
6 cloud ear mushrooms, soaked in ½ cup hot water 15 minutes, stems discarded, caps halved
6 Chinese dried black mushrooms, soaked in ½ cup hot water 15 minutes, stems discarded, caps thinly sliced
1 tablespoon soy sauce
¼ teaspoon sugar
¾ teaspoon salt
2 tablespoons cornstarch mixed with 3 tablespoons water
1 egg, beaten until slightly foamy
3 tablespoons Chinese red vinegar
½ teaspoon ground white pepper
2 green onions including tops, thinly sliced

Bring chicken stock to boil in uncovered wok at 250°. Add pork, tofu, bamboo shoots, cloud ear and Chinese mushrooms; cook 3 to 5 minutes. Mix soy sauce, sugar, salt and cornstarch mixture; add to soup; stir; cook until soup just comes to a boil. Slowly swirl in egg; turn wok OFF. Put vinegar and pepper in bowl; add soup and green onions. Stir; serve immediately.

## Hot Oriental Mushroom Soup

Makes 4 to 6 servings
Preparation Time: 30 minutes

4 cups chicken stock
6 Chinese dried black mushrooms, soaked in hot water 20 minutes, drained, stems discarded, caps thinly sliced
¼ cup Madeira
Chopped green onion

Bring stock to boil in uncovered wok at 250°. Add mushrooms and wine; reduce heat to "simmer" and cover; simmer 20 minutes. Sprinkle with green onion; serve immediately.

# Rice and Noodles

## Stir-Fried Noodles

Makes 4 servings
Preparation Time: 20 minutes; 2 to 3 minutes to cook

3 tablespoons peanut oil
1 1-inch piece fresh gingerroot, peeled and finely chopped
6 Chinese dried black mushrooms, soaked in hot water 20 minutes, drained, stems discarded, caps thinly sliced
3 green onions, thinly sliced
½ teaspoon salt
8 ounces Chinese noodles, cooked and drained
2 tablespoons soy sauce
1 teaspoon sesame oil
1 tablespoon dry sherry

Heat oil in uncovered wok at 375°. Add next 4 ingredients; stir-fry 30 seconds. Add remaining ingredients; stir-fry to combine and heat. Serve immediately.

## Subgum Fried Rice

Makes 4 servings
Preparation Time: 15 minutes; 5 minutes to cook

2 tablespoons peanut oil
¼ cup thinly sliced green onions including tops
¼ cup frozen peas
¼ cup diced cooked shrimp
¼ cup diced cooked lean ham
2 eggs, lightly beaten
½ teaspoon salt
2 cups cold cooked rice
2 tablespoons soy sauce

Heat oil in uncovered wok at 325°. Add onions; stir-fry 30 seconds. Add next 3 ingredients; stir-fry 1 minute. Push to one side of wok; add eggs; sprinkle with salt; scramble; cut apart with spatula; mix in with other ingredients. Add rice and soy sauce; stir-fry to mix and heat through, about 2 minutes. Serve immediately.

# Rice and Noodles

## Red Pepper Rice

Makes 4 servings
Preparation Time: 20 minutes; 20 minutes to cook

3 tablespoons olive oil
4 cloves garlic, peeled, split lengthwise
2 onions, peeled and chopped
Pinch dried red pepper flakes
1 cup long-grain rice
½ small red pepper, cored, seeded and diced
1 small tomato, cored, peeled and chopped
1½ cups chicken stock
Salt to taste

Heat oil in uncovered wok at 350°. Add garlic; swirl around in hot oil 30 seconds; remove and discard. Add onions; stir-fry 1 minute. Add pepper flakes; stir-fry 10 seconds. Add rice; stir-fry 2 to 3 minutes or until all grains are coated with oil. Add next 3 ingredients; stir and bring to boil. Cover; reduce heat to "simmer" for 15 minutes. Fluff rice with fork; season with salt. Serve immediately.

## Fried Rice with Ham

Makes 4 servings
Preparation Time: 15 minutes; 5 minutes to cook

2 tablespoons peanut oil
⅓ cup thinly sliced green onions including tops
½ teaspoon peeled and minced fresh gingerroot
½ teaspoon minced garlic
2 eggs, lightly beaten
¼ teaspoon salt
¼ teaspoon sugar
⅓ pound finely diced cooked lean ham
½ cup frozen tiny peas
2 tablespoons soy sauce
2 cups cold cooked rice
½ teaspoon sesame oil

Heat oil in uncovered wok at 325°. Add next 3 ingredients; stir-fry 1 minute. Add eggs; scramble loosely; break up with spatula. Add next 5 ingredients; stir-fry 2 minutes. Add rice; stir-fry 30 seconds. Add sesame oil; stir and serve immediately.

**Note:** Leftover fried rice can be refrigerated and reheated as well as frozen, thawed and reheated. For best results with fried rice recipes, be sure rice is cold before stir-frying.

Flavored Rice, page 24
Fried Rice with Ham, this page

# Rice and Noodles

## Pork Fried Rice

Makes 4 servings
Preparation Time: 15 minutes; 7 minutes to cook

2 tablespoons peanut oil
½ pound lean pork, cut in thin strips
½ teaspoon sugar
½ teaspoon salt
½ cup thinly sliced green onions including tops
½ cup thinly sliced celery
2 cups cold cooked rice
1 cup fresh bean sprouts
3 tablespoons soy sauce
3 eggs, lightly beaten

Heat oil in uncovered wok at 350°. Add next 3 ingredients; stir-fry 2 to 3 minutes. Add green onions and celery; stir-fry 1 minute. Add rice and bean sprouts; stir-fry 30 seconds. Add soy sauce; stir to mix. Make well in center of rice; pour in beaten eggs; allow to set; scramble with spatula; stir into rice. Serve immediately.

## Exotic Noodles

Makes 4 servings
Preparation Time: 15 minutes

¼ cup unsalted butter
½ pound Chinese egg noodles, cooked and drained
¼ cup toasted sesame seed
¼ cup soy sauce
2 green onions, thinly sliced

Melt butter in wok at 325°. (Do not use higher temperature or butter will burn.) Add next 3 ingredients; toss to combine; heat through. Sprinkle with green onions. Serve immediately.

## Flavored Rice

Makes 4 servings
Preparation Time: 10 minutes; 5 minutes to cook

1 tablespoon sesame oil
3 tablespoons toasted sesame seed
3 green onions, minced
2 cloves garlic, peeled and crushed
1½ cups fresh bean sprouts
2 cups hot cooked rice
2 tablespoons soy sauce

Heat oil in uncovered wok at 350°. Add next 3 ingredients; stir-fry until onions soften, about 1 minute. Add bean sprouts; stir-fry until heated through. Add rice and soy sauce; toss to combine. Heat through. Serve immediately.

# Rice and Noodles

## Vegetarian Fried Rice

Makes 4 to 6 servings
Preparation Time: 10 minutes; 5 minutes to cook

2 tablespoons peanut oil
½ teaspoon salt
2 eggs, lightly beaten
⅔ cup thinly sliced green onions
1 cup fresh bean sprouts
3 tablespoons soy sauce
3 cups cold cooked rice
Freshly ground black pepper to taste

Heat oil in uncovered wok at 350°. Add salt and eggs; scramble quickly, breaking into small pieces with spatula. Add onions; stir-fry 2 minutes. Add bean sprouts; stir-fry 1 minute. Add soy sauce, rice and pepper; stir-fry until heated through, about 1 minute. Serve immediately.

## Noodle Salad with Oriental Dressing

Makes 4 servings
Preparation Time: 20 minutes

½ pound thin egg noodles or linguine
Oriental Dressing
1 cup fresh bean sprouts
2 cups shredded lettuce
3 tablespoons sesame seed

Cook noodles in boiling salted water in wok at 250° until al dente or just tender; drain; toss with Dressing to prevent sticking. Just before serving, toss noodles with bean sprouts and lettuce. Sprinkle with sesame seed; serve immediately.

### Oriental Dressing

2 tablespoons peanut butter
2 tablespoons water
2 tablespoons soy sauce
2 tablespoons vinegar
2 tablespoons peanut oil
1 tablespoon sesame oil
2 tablespoons minced green onion tops
½ teaspoon minced garlic
½ teaspoon peeled and minced fresh gingerroot
1 teaspoon salt

Combine all ingredients in jar; cover; shake to combine.

# Rice and Noodles

## Sticky Rice

Makes 3 cups
Preparation Time: 20 minutes

**2 cups cold water**
**1 teaspoon salt**
**1 cup short-grain rice**

Bring water to boil in wok at 225°; add salt and rice; stir. Reduce heat to 200°; cover; cook 15 minutes or until water has evaporated.

## Shrimp Fried Rice

Makes 4 servings
Preparation Time: 15 minutes; 7 minutes to cook

**2 tablespoons peanut oil**
**½ pound small shrimp, shelled**
**½ teaspoon sugar**
**½ teaspoon salt**
**½ cup thinly sliced green onions including tops**
**½ cup diced bamboo shoots**
**2 cups cold cooked rice**
**1 cup fresh bean sprouts**
**3 tablespoons soy sauce**
**3 eggs, lightly beaten**

Heat oil in uncovered wok at 375°. Add next 3 ingredients; stir-fry 2 to 3 minutes. Add green onions and bamboo shoots; stir-fry 1 minute. Add rice and bean sprouts; stir-fry 30 seconds. Add soy sauce; stir to mix. Make well in center of rice; pour in eggs; allow to set; scramble with spatula; stir into rice. Serve immediately.

## Sesame Rice

Makes 4 servings
Preparation Time: 20 minutes

**1 tablespoon unsalted butter**
**1 tablespoon peanut oil**
**1 cup raw long-grain rice**
**¼ cup sesame seed**
**2 cups chicken stock**
**1 teaspoon salt**
**¼ teaspoon peeled and minced fresh gingerroot**
**1 tablespoon soy sauce** or more to taste

Melt butter in oil in uncovered wok at 325°. Add rice and sesame seed; cook, stirring constantly, until light brown. Add stock, salt and gingerroot. Stir; bring to boil; cover; reduce heat to "simmer" for 15 minutes. Uncover; stir in soy sauce. Serve immediately.

# Rice and Noodles

## Spanish Rice

Makes 6 to 8 servings
Preparation Time: 40 minutes

4 cups chicken stock
1 cup tomato sauce
1 teaspoon salt
1 tablespoon whole
  pickling spice
2 cups long-grain rice
2 tablespoons oil
  Chopped fresh tomato
  Chopped fresh green
  pepper

Mix first 3 ingredients in wok. Place pickling spice in cheesecloth bag; add to wok. Bring to boil at 225°; reduce heat to "simmer" for 10 minutes. Sauté rice in hot oil in skillet or another wok at 325° until lightly browned. Add to stock mixture. Bring to boil at 225°; cover; reduce to "simmer" for about 25 minutes or until rice is tender. Remove spice bag. Serve immediately garnished with chopped tomato and pepper.

## Spicy Noodles and Ham

Makes 6 servings
Preparation Time: 5 minutes; 2 minutes to cook

1½ quarts water
½ teaspoon salt
1 pound Chinese egg
  noodles
1 teaspoon sesame oil
3 tablespoons soy sauce
1½ tablespoons vinegar
1 teaspoon sugar
½ teaspoon hot pepper
  sauce
3 tablespoons chopped
  green onion
½ cup chicken stock
1 cup shredded cooked ham

Bring water and salt to boil in wok at 250°. Add noodles; boil 2 minutes, stirring constantly. Drain; rinse under cold running water to stop cooking. Drain; pour into bowl; stir in sesame oil. Mix next 6 ingredients; pour over noodles; toss to combine. Add ham; toss. Serve cold or at room temperature.

# Tofu

## Stir-Fried Tofu and Vegetables

Makes 4 servings
Preparation Time: 10 minutes; 5 minutes to cook

2 tablespoons peanut oil
1 clove garlic, peeled and crushed
¼ pound fresh mushrooms, wiped clean and thinly sliced
1 carrot, pared and cut in thin diagonal slices
1 onion, peeled, halved and thinly sliced
1 green pepper, cored, seeded and cut in ½-inch pieces
3 tablespoons soy sauce
½ teaspoon sugar

1 pound tofu, cut in ½-inch cubes
1 teaspoon cornstarch mixed with 2 teaspoons cold water

Heat oil in uncovered wok at 350°. Add garlic and mushrooms; stir-fry 30 seconds. Add next 3 ingredients; stir-fry 2 minutes. Add soy sauce, sugar and tofu; stir-fry 10 seconds. Cover; cook 1 minute. Uncover; stir cornstarch mixture; add to wok. Stir-fry until slightly thickened. Serve immediately.

## Fried Tofu

Makes 4 servings
Preparation Time: 20 minutes

1 pound tofu
¼ teaspoon salt
3 eggs, lightly beaten
¼ cup flour
2 tablespoons water
Peanut oil
¼ teaspoon crushed fresh gingerroot
1 green onion including top, finely chopped
1 tablespoon soy sauce

Cut tofu in half horizontally; sprinkle with salt; let stand 10 minutes. Pat dry; cut tofu in 1 x 2-inch pieces. Mix next 3 ingredients in bowl until smooth. Heat 1 tablespoon oil in uncovered wok at 375°. Dip tofu pieces, one at a time, in batter; fry, three to four at a time, in oil until golden brown; drain. (Add more oil if necessary.) Heat 2 tablespoons oil in wok. Add gingerroot and green onion; stir-fry 10 seconds. Return tofu to wok with soy sauce; cover; cook 1 minute. Serve immediately.

## Scrambled Tofu

Makes 4 servings
Preparation Time: 5 minutes; 4 minutes to cook

1½ tablespoons peanut oil
1 pound tofu, cut in ½-inch cubes
Juice of ½ lemon
Salt and freshly ground black pepper to taste
1 medium onion, peeled, halved, and thinly sliced
½ pound snow peas, ends and strings removed
½ teaspoon dried thyme

Heat oil in uncovered wok at 350°. Add tofu; gently stir-fry 2 minutes. Add remaining ingredients; stir-fry 2 minutes. Serve immediately.

## Spicy Tofu

Makes 4 servings
Preparation Time: 5 minutes; 4 minutes to cook

3 tablespoons hot bean paste
1 tablespoon dry sherry
1 teaspoon sesame oil
2 tablespoons peanut oil
1 teaspoon salt
2 onions, peeled, halved and thinly sliced
1 pound tofu, cut in ½-inch cubes

Mix first 3 ingredients; set aside. Heat oil in uncovered wok at 350°. Add salt and onions; stir-fry 2 minutes. Add tofu; gently stir-fry 1 minute. Add bean paste mixture; stir-fry to coat. Serve immediately.

## Tofu with Oyster Sauce

Makes 4 servings
Preparation Time: 5 minutes; 4 minutes to cook

2 tablespoons peanut oil
½ teaspoon minced garlic
2 green onions, thinly sliced
½ pound tofu, cut in ½-inch cubes
½ cup chicken stock
2 tablespoons oyster sauce
1 teaspoon cornstarch mixed with 2 teaspoons cold water

Heat oil in uncovered wok at 350°. Add garlic and green onions; stir-fry 30 seconds. Add tofu; gently stir-fry 1 minute. Add stock and oyster sauce; cover; cook 1 minute. Uncover; stir cornstarch mixture; add to wok; stir until slightly thickened. Serve immediately.

# Tempura

## TEMPURA

Tempura is a Japanese frying technique in which small pieces or slices of food are dipped in a thin batter and fried in hot oil in a wok. The result is tender-crisp vegetables, seafood and meat encased in a delicate crunchy coating. The food can be cooked by one or two people in the kitchen just before serving, or the cooking can be done in the electric wok at the table. A variety of garnishes and dipping sauces are served.

## Batter I

2 eggs
1⅓ cups flour
1 teaspoon salt
1 cup flat beer

Beat eggs in bowl; add ⅓ cup flour and salt. Add beer alternately with remaining flour, beating after each addition. Let batter stand at room temperature 1 hour.

## Batter II

⅔ cup flour
3 tablespoons cornstarch
½ teaspoon salt
2 eggs
¾ cup ice water

Stir first 3 ingredients together in bowl. Beat eggs and ice water in another bowl until blended. Add to flour mixture; stir until just moistened. Batter will be lumpy. Do not stir again. Keep batter cold by placing it in a bowl set in a larger bowl of crushed ice.

## Suggested Ingredients:

Sweet potato, peeled, cut in ¼-inch-wide slices
Spanish onion, peeled, cut in ¼-inch-wide slices without separating into rings
Green or red pepper, cut in ½-inch-wide strips
Zucchini, unpeeled, cut in ⅛-inch-wide strips
Green beans, ends trimmed
Cucumber, peeled, thinly sliced
Parsley sprigs
Mushrooms, halved if particularly large
Eggplant, unpeeled, cut in thin strips
Celery, cut in 3-inch-long strips
Carrot, cut in 3-inch-long strips
Snow peas, ends and strings removed

Shrimp Tempura

# Tempura

Flounder or sole, cut in 2-inch pieces
Sea scallops, halved if particularly large
Shrimp, shelled except for tails, deveined
Chunks of lobster, 1½ inches
Chunks of boneless, skinned chicken breast, ½ inch
Chicken livers, halved

**Dipping Sauces and Seasonings:**

Sweet and Sour Sauce (Recipe on page 43)
Hot Mustard Sauce (Recipe on page 44)
Plum Sauce (Recipe on page 43)
Tempura Sauce (Recipe on page 44)

Soy sauce
Grated white radish
Lemon juice

**To Prepare Tempura:**

1. Have all foods for tempura frying cut in bite-size or thin strips, arranged attractively on a platter. Be sure foods are dry and at room temperature before cooking.

2. Prepare the dipping sauces and seasonings to be served. These can be prepared hours in advance. They should be at room temperature when served.

3. Prepare either Batter I (it must stand at room temperature 1 hour) or Batter II (it must be prepared just before using and kept cold) or prepare both batters, if desired.

4. Heat 3 cups peanut oil in uncovered wok at 375°. Do not add more than 3 cups of oil to wok. Fit the wok with a tempura ring if available. If not, line a plate with paper towels for draining excess oil from foods.

5. Using tongs, fork or chopsticks, coat foods to be fried, one by one, with batter; drop into hot oil. Fry 3 or 4 items at a time, browning on all sides, 2 to 3 minutes. Remove cooked food with slotted spoon or strainer; place on tempura ring or paper towels to drain; serve while hot.

6. Each person dips the tempura-fried foods in the desired sauces. Food can be cooked by one person or everyone at the table. Divide batter so that each person has his own dish. If using the batter containing ice water, place individual bowls of this batter in bowls of crushed ice to keep it cold.

## CHINESE HOT POT

A Chinese hot pot dinner is a fun way to entertain. To be authentic, a Mongolian hot pot should be used, but the electric wok will serve the purpose perfectly well. Chicken stock is heated to boiling in the wok. Guests then dip meat, seafood and vegetables into the stock using chopsticks or spearing food on bamboo skewers. These foods are then eaten with an assortment of sauces.

Then cellophane noodles are cooked in the stock, and the noodles and stock are ladled into serving bowls as the last course of the dinner. All of the preparation is done in advance, making this an almost effortless party menu. It's best to serve this to no more than four people at a time so each will have easy access to the wok.

**Suggested Vegetables:**

Broccoli flowerets, sliced ¼ inch thick
Cauliflowerets, sliced ¼ inch thick
Carrots, pared, cut in ⅛-inch-thick diagonal slices
Snow peas, ends and strings removed
Spinach leaves, washed, stems removed
Mushrooms, wiped clean, sliced ¼ inch thick
Green onions, roots removed, cut in 1½-inch-long pieces
Red or green pepper strips, ¼ inch wide

**Suggested Proteins:**

Pork tenderloin, beef top sirloin, lean lamb; all cut across grain in
⅛-inch-thick slices
Chicken breast, skinned and boned, cut across grain in
¼-inch-thick slices
Chicken livers, halved
Medium to large shrimp, shelled and deveined, halved lengthwise
Sea scallops, halved if particularly large
Tofu or bean curd, cut in ½- to 1-inch cubes

**Other Ingredients:**

3 to 4 ounces cellophane noodles
3 to 4 cups warm water
6 to 8 cups chicken stock
Soy sauce
Hoisin Sauce

Teriyaki Sauce (Recipe on page 43)
Plum Sauce (Recipe on page 43)
Hot Mustard Sauce (Recipe on
page 44)

**TO PREPARE HOT POT**

Arrange vegetables and proteins attractively in overlapping layers on serving trays. Cover; refrigerate until serving time. Cover cellophane noodles with warm water; let stand 30 minutes. Drain; cut in 6-inch lengths. When ready to serve, put 6 to 8 cups stock in wok. Heat to boiling at 250°. Let guests cook vegetables and proteins to desired doneness, 1 to 4 minutes. Serve with dipping sauces. It may be necessary to add additional stock to wok. As the last course, heat noodles in stock; ladle into bowls.

# Vegetables

## Vegetable Stir-Fry Deluxe

Makes 6 servings
Preparation Time: 20 minutes; 7 minutes to cook

- 2 tablespoons peanut oil
- 2 onions, peeled, halved vertically and sliced
- 2 green peppers, cored, seeded and cut in thin strips
- 2 carrots, pared and cut in thin diagonal slices
- 2 ribs celery, cut in thin diagonal slices
- 1 ¼-inch slice fresh gingerroot, peeled and minced
- 3 cloves garlic, peeled and finely chopped
- 2 tablespoons soy sauce
- 2 tablespoons dry sherry
- 1 pound broccoli flowerets, blanched 3 minutes
- ½ pound cauliflowerets, blanched 3 minutes
- 1 cup shredded bok choy (Chinese cabbage)
- 1 cup fresh bean sprouts
- 2 tablespoons fresh lemon juice
  Salt and freshly ground black pepper to taste

Heat oil in uncovered wok at 375°. Add next 3 ingredients; stir-fry 3 minutes. Add next 5 ingredients; stir-fry 2 minutes. Add broccoli and cauliflower; stir-fry 1 minute. Add cabbage; stir-fry 30 seconds. Add bean sprouts and lemon juice; stir-fry to heat through. Season with salt and pepper. Serve immediately.

## Broccoli and Cauliflower with Garlic

Makes 4 servings
Preparation Time: 10 minutes; 5 minutes to cook

- 2 tablespoons peanut oil
- 2 small cloves garlic, peeled and crushed
- 2 cups small broccoli flowerets, blanched 3 minutes
- 2 cups small cauliflowerets, blanched 3 minutes
- 1 cup chicken stock
- 2 teaspoons cornstarch mixed with 2 teaspoons cold water

Heat oil in uncovered wok at 350°. Add garlic; stir-fry 30 seconds. Add broccoli and cauliflower; stir-fry 2 minutes. Add stock; cover; cook 2 minutes or until vegetables are tender-crisp. Stir cornstarch mixture; add to wok; stir-fry until sauce thickens slightly. Serve immediately.

Ginger Stir-Fried Vegetables, page 36
Vegetable Stir-Fry Deluxe, this page

# Vegetables

## Ginger Stir-Fried Vegetables

Makes 4 servings
Preparation Time: 10 minutes; 5 minutes to cook

- 2 tablespoons peanut oil
- 1 teaspoon peeled and minced fresh gingerroot
- 1 clove garlic, peeled and minced
- ¼ pound cauliflowerets, cut in ¼-inch slices
- 1 cup pared and thinly sliced carrots
- ⅓ cup chicken stock
- ¼ pound asparagus, cut in 1½-inch pieces
- ¼ pound snow peas, ends and strings removed
- ½ teaspoon salt
- ½ teaspoon sesame oil

Heat oil in uncovered wok at 350°. Add gingerroot and garlic; stir-fry 30 seconds. Add cauliflower, carrots and chicken stock; cover; cook 2 minutes. Uncover; add asparagus; cover; cook 1 minute. Uncover; add snow peas; stir-fry 30 seconds. Add salt and sesame oil; stir-fry 30 seconds. Serve immediately.

## Green Beans with Water Chestnuts

Makes 4 servings
Preparation Time: 15 minutes; 8 minutes to cook

- 1 teaspoon peanut oil
- 1 teaspoon sesame oil
- ½ pound green beans, cut diagonally in 1½-inch pieces
- ½ cup sliced water chestnuts, drained
- ½ cup sliced fresh mushrooms
- 1 small clove garlic, peeled and crushed
- 2 tablespoons soy sauce
- 2 tablespoons cold water
- ½ teaspoon salt
- ¼ teaspoon freshly ground black pepper
- 2 teaspoons sesame seed

Heat both oils in uncovered wok at 350°. Add next 4 ingredients; stir-fry 1 minute. Add remaining ingredients; cover; cook until beans are tender, 5 to 7 minutes. Serve immediately.

# Vegetables

## Harvest Vegetable Stir-Fry

Makes 6 to 8 servings
Preparation Time: 15 minutes; 10 minutes to cook

2 tablespoons peanut oil
1 ¼-inch slice fresh
   gingerroot, peeled
2 cups small broccoli
   flowerets, blanched 3
   minutes
2 cups small cauliflowerets,
   blanched 3 minutes
2 cups sliced fresh
   mushrooms
1 green pepper, cored,
   seeded and cut in ¼-inch-
   wide strips
2 cups thin diagonal celery
   slices
1 large clove garlic, peeled
   and minced
1 teaspoon salt

1 teaspoon freshly ground
   black pepper
2 tablespoons soy sauce
½ cup grated sharp Cheddar
   cheese

Heat oil in uncovered wok at 325°. Add gingerroot; swirl around sides of wok; discard. Add broccoli, cauliflower, mushrooms, green pepper and celery in that order. Add garlic, salt and pepper. Cover; cook 5 minutes or until vegetables are tender-crisp. Add soy sauce; toss. Sprinkle with cheese; cook until cheese melts. Serve immediately.

## Stir-Fried Peppers

Makes 4 servings
Preparation Time: 15 minutes; 7 minutes to cook

2 tablespoons olive oil
2 green peppers, cored,
   seeded, cut in ½-inch-
   wide lengthwise strips
2 red peppers, cored,
   seeded, cut in ½-inch-
   wide lengthwise strips
1 large clove garlic, peeled
   and crushed
1 medium onion, peeled,
   thinly sliced and
   separated into rings
½ teaspoon crumbled
   oregano
   Pinch cayenne pepper

3 to 4 dashes hot pepper
   sauce
   Salt and freshly ground
   black pepper to taste

Heat oil in uncovered wok at 350°. Add pepper strips; stir-fry 2 minutes. Add remaining ingredients; stir-fry 30 seconds. Cover; simmer 3 to 4 minutes or until peppers are tender-crisp. Serve immediately.

**Note:** If red peppers are not available, substitute green peppers.

# Vegetables

## Cauliflower Stir-Fry

Makes 4 servings
Preparation Time: 5 minutes; 10 minutes to cook

3 tablespoons peanut oil
1 small head cauliflower, separated into small flowerets
3 tablespoons fresh lemon juice
3 tablespoons water
4 green onions, thinly sliced
1 clove garlic, peeled and crushed
   Salt and freshly ground white pepper to taste

Heat 1 tablespoon oil in uncovered wok at 250°. Add next 3 ingredients; cover; cook 5 to 7 minutes or until tender-crisp. Remove from wok with strainer; set aside. Heat remaining 2 tablespoons oil in wok at 325°. Add green onions; stir-fry 30 seconds. Add garlic; stir-fry 30 seconds. Add cauliflower, salt and pepper. Stir-fry 1 minute. Serve immediately.

## Garden Stir-Fry

Makes 4 servings
Preparation Time: 20 minutes; 8 minutes to cook

2 tablespoons peanut oil
½ pound fresh mushrooms, wiped clean, thinly sliced
   Salt and freshly ground black pepper to taste
1 tablespoon fresh lemon juice
2 small onions, peeled, halved vertically and sliced
1 large green pepper, cored, seeded and cut in thin strips
2 large cloves garlic, peeled and crushed
1 teaspoon dried rosemary, crumbled
1 teaspoon dried basil
½ teaspoon dried marjoram
   Salt and freshly ground black pepper to taste

2 tablespoons dry red wine
2 medium unpeeled zucchini, cut in thin diagonal slices
2 small tomatoes, cored, each cut in 6 wedges

Heat 1 tablespoon oil in uncovered wok at 350°. Add mushrooms; sprinkle with salt and pepper to taste and lemon juice. Stir-fry 2 minutes; remove; set aside. Heat remaining 1 tablespoon oil in wok at 350°. Add next 3 ingredients; stir-fry 2 minutes. Add seasonings, wine, zucchini, tomatoes and mushrooms; stir-fry 2 minutes. Serve immediately.

## Bean Sprout and Mushroom Stir-Fry

Makes 4 servings
Preparation Time: 20 minutes; 6 minutes to cook

2 tablespoons peanut oil
6 to 8 Chinese dried black mushrooms, soaked in hot water 20 minutes, drained, stems discarded, caps thinly sliced
3½ cups fresh bean sprouts
1 clove garlic, peeled and finely chopped
1 teaspoon peeled and finely chopped fresh gingerroot
½ cup water
2 teaspoons cornstarch mixed with 1 tablespoon cold water
1 tablespoon soy sauce
2 green onions, cut in 1-inch pieces

Heat oil in uncovered wok at 350°. Add mushrooms, bean sprouts, garlic and gingerroot; stir-fry 2 minutes. Add water; bring to boil. Stir cornstarch mixture; add to wok with soy sauce. Stir until thickened. Garnish with green onions. Serve immediately.

## Stir-Fried Asparagus

Makes 4 servings
Preparation Time: 10 minutes; 6 minutes to cook

2 tablespoons peanut oil
2 cloves garlic, peeled and minced
1 pound asparagus, cut in 2-inch diagonal pieces, leaving tips whole
1 cup chicken stock
2 tablespoons dry sherry
2 tablespoons soy sauce
2 teaspoons cornstarch
¼ teaspoon sugar
¾ teaspoon salt
¼ teaspoon black pepper

Heat oil in uncovered wok at 250°. Add garlic; stir-fry 10 seconds. Add asparagus and stock; bring to boil. Cover; cook 5 minutes or until asparagus is tender-crisp. Meanwhile, mix remaining ingredients. Uncover; stir cornstarch mixture; add to wok; stir-fry until sauce thickens. Serve immediately.

# Vegetables

## Stir-Fried Spinach

Makes 3 to 4 servings
Preparation Time: 10 minutes; 3 minutes to cook

2 tablespoons peanut oil
1 clove garlic, peeled
1 pound fresh spinach, washed, stems discarded
½ teaspoon salt
Pinch sugar

Heat oil in uncovered wok at 350°. Add garlic and spinach; stir-fry 1 minute. Discard garlic. Add salt and sugar; stir-fry 1 minute. Serve immediately.

## Snow Peas with Water Chestnuts

Makes 4 servings
Preparation Time: 10 minutes; 2 minutes to cook

2 tablespoons peanut oil
1 ¼-inch slice fresh gingerroot, peeled
1 pound snow peas, ends and strings removed
1 teaspoon salt
1 tablespoon water
1 8-ounce can sliced water chestnuts, drained
½ teaspoon sugar

Heat oil in uncovered wok at 375°. Add gingerroot; swirl around wok 30 seconds; discard. Add snow peas; stir-fry 30 seconds. Add salt and water; cover; cook 30 seconds. Uncover; add water chestnuts and sugar; stir-fry 30 seconds. Serve immediately.

## Sweet and Sour Zucchini

Makes 4 servings
Preparation Time: 10 minutes; 10 minutes to cook

2 tablespoons peanut oil
3 unpeeled medium zucchini, cut in ½-inch slices
2 tablespoons sugar dissolved in 2 tablespoons vinegar
Salt and freshly ground white pepper to taste

Heat oil in uncovered wok at 375°. Add zucchini; stir-fry until tender-crisp. Add remaining ingredients; simmer 3 minutes. Serve immediately.

# Vegetables

## Stir-Fried Broccoli and Carrots

Makes 6 servings
Preparation Time: 15 minutes; 5 minutes to cook

2 tablespoons peanut oil
2 ¼-inch slices gingerroot, peeled and finely chopped
1 clove garlic, peeled and finely chopped
1½ cups small broccoli flowerets
1½ cups pared and thinly sliced carrots
1 small onion, peeled, sliced and separated into rings
¾ cup chicken stock
1 teaspoon salt
1 tablespoon cornstarch mixed with 2 tablespoons cold water
1 8-ounce can sliced water chestnuts, drained
1 cup sliced fresh mushrooms
2 tablespoons oyster sauce

Heat oil in uncovered wok at 350°. Add gingerroot and garlic; stir-fry 15 seconds. Add next 3 ingredients; stir-fry 1 minute. Add chicken stock and salt; cover; cook until carrots are tender-crisp, about 3 minutes. Stir cornstarch mixture; add to vegetable mixture. Cook, stirring, until slightly thickened, about 10 seconds. Add remaining ingredients; stir-fry 30 seconds. Serve immediately.

## Stir-Fried Green Beans

Makes 4 servings
Preparation Time: 10 minutes; 4 minutes to cook

2 tablespoons peanut oil
2 small cloves garlic, peeled and finely chopped
2 ¼-inch slices fresh gingerroot, peeled and finely chopped
2 green onions, thinly sliced
1 pound green beans, ends removed, blanched 4 minutes
  Salt to taste

Heat oil in uncovered wok at 350°. Add next 3 ingredients; stir-fry 30 seconds. Add beans; stir-fry 2 to 3 minutes or until tender-crisp. Add salt. Serve immediately.

41

# Sauces

## Plum Sauce

Makes approximately 1 cup
Preparation Time: 15 minutes

- **1 cup plum jam, jelly or preserves**
- **½ cup applesauce**
- **½ teaspoon ground ginger**
- **2 teaspoons cornstarch**
- **2 teaspoons soy sauce**
- **2 teaspoons wine vinegar**

Mix plum jam and applesauce in wok; bring to boil at 225°. Combine ginger, cornstarch, soy sauce, vinegar; stir into jam mixture. Cook, stirring constantly, until mixture thickens. Cool. Refrigerate until serving time. Bring to room temperature before serving.

## Sweet and Sour Sauce

Makes approximately 1¼ cups
Preparation Time: 5 minutes

- **½ cup pineapple juice**
- **½ cup white wine vinegar**
- **2 tablespoons peanut oil**
- **2 tablespoons packed light brown sugar**
- **1 tablespoon soy sauce**
- **½ teaspoon freshly ground black pepper**

- **2 teaspoons cornstarch mixed with 4 teaspoons cold water**

Mix first 6 ingredients in wok; bring to boil at 225°. Stir cornstarch mixture; add to wok, stirring until sauce is clear and slightly thickened.

## Teriyaki Sauce

Makes approximately ⅔ cup
Preparation Time: 10 minutes

- **½ cup pineapple juice**
- **¼ cup packed light brown sugar**
- **2 tablespoons soy sauce**
- **1 tablespoon peanut oil**
- **¾ teaspoon ground ginger**
- **¼ teaspoon salt**
- **1 clove garlic, peeled and minced**

Mix all ingredients in wok; heat to blend flavors at "simmer" setting.

Clockwise, from top: Plum Sauce, this page
Sweet and Sour Sauce, this page; Hot Mustard Sauce, page 44

# Sauces

## Ginger Sauce

Makes approximately ¾ cup
Preparation Time: 2 minutes

1 **tablespoon ground ginger**
1 **small clove garlic, peeled and crushed**
¼ **cup water**
2 **tablespoons sugar**
½ **cup soy sauce**

Mix all ingredients. Use as dipping sauce.

## Tempura Sauce

Makes approximately ½ cup
Preparation Time: 10 minutes

¼ **cup chicken stock**
1 **tablespoon soy sauce**
1 **tablespoon cream sherry**
1 **tablespoon grated daikon (Japanese radish)**
1 **tablespoon peeled and grated fresh gingerroot**

Combine first 3 ingredients. Just before serving, stir in daikon and gingerroot.

## Hot Mustard Sauce

Makes 1 cup
Preparation Time: 15 minutes

¼ **cup dry mustard**
2 **tablespoons peanut oil**
2 **tablespoons water**
¼ **cup sugar**
1 **tablespoon cornstarch**
½ **teaspoon salt**
½ **cup water**
¼ **cup white vinegar**

Mix mustard and oil in small bowl. Gradually add 2 tablespoons water, stirring constantly, to form smooth paste. Stir together sugar, cornstarch and salt in wok; gradually add ½ cup water and vinegar. Blend thoroughly. Cook at 225°, stirring constantly, until mixture thickens. Gradually add to mustard mixture, stirring constantly, until blended. Refrigerate until serving time. Stir before serving. Serve at room temperature.

# Beef

## Stir-Fried Broccoli and Beef

Makes 4 servings
Preparation Time: 15 minutes; 8 minutes to cook

2 **teaspoons dry sherry**
⅛ **teaspoon freshly ground black pepper**
2 **teaspoons soy sauce**
½ **teaspoon salt**
½ **teaspoon sugar**
¾ **cup water**
2 **teaspoons cornstarch**
¼ **cup peanut oil**
¾ **pound broccoli, flowerets removed and reserved; stalks cut diagonally into ¼-inch slices**
½ **pound flank steak, thinly sliced across grain and cut in 1½-inch-long strips**

Mix first 5 ingredients and ½ cup water; set aside. Mix cornstarch with remaining ¼ cup water; set aside. Heat 2 tablespoons oil in uncovered wok at 300°. Add broccoli stalk slices; cover; cook 2 minutes. Add flowerets; cover; cook 2 minutes or until tender-crisp. Remove broccoli to hot platter. Add remaining 2 tablespoons oil to wok; heat at 375°. Add meat; stir-fry 1 minute. Add soy sauce mixture; stir-fry 2 minutes. Return broccoli to wok; mix. Add cornstarch mixture; stir until slightly thickened. Serve immediately.

## Mongolian Beef

Makes 4 servings
Preparation Time: 15 minutes; 4½ minutes to cook

1 **pound lean flank** or **sirloin steak, thinly sliced across grain and cut in 1½-inch-long strips**
2 **tablespoons soy sauce**
½ **teaspoon salt**
1 **tablespoon dry sherry**
½ **teaspoon dried red pepper flakes**
3 **tablespoons peanut oil**
1 **tablespoon sesame oil**
½ **teaspoon chopped garlic**
1 **bunch green onions, each cut in half lengthwise, then cut diagonally in 1-inch-long pieces**

Put meat strips in bowl; add 1 tablespoon soy sauce, next 3 ingredients and 2 tablespoons oil; set aside. Mix remaining 1 tablespoon soy sauce with sesame oil; set aside. Heat remaining 1 tablespoon oil in uncovered wok at 400°. Add garlic; stir-fry 10 seconds. Add beef; stir-fry 2 minutes. Add onion and sesame oil mixture; stir-fry until heated through, 1 to 2 minutes. Serve immediately.

## Oriental Beef with Vegetables

Makes 4 servings
Preparation Time: 15 minutes; 9 minutes to cook

1 **pound lean flank** or
**sirloin steak, thinly sliced**
**across grain and cut in**
**1½-inch-long strips**
2 **tablespoons peanut oil**
2 **tablespoons soy sauce**
2 **tablespoons dry sherry**
½ **teaspoon sugar**
1 **clove garlic, peeled and**
**crushed**
½ **teaspoon peeled and**
**finely grated fresh**
**gingerroot**
2 **teaspoons cornstarch**
2 **tablespoons water**
3 **tablespoons peanut oil**
1 **small onion, peeled,**
**halved and thinly sliced**
1 **small green pepper,**
**cored, seeded and cut in**
**thin 1½-inch long strips**

1 **small red pepper, cored,**
**seeded and cut in thin**
**1½-inch-long strips**
½ **cup sliced bamboo**
**shoots, drained**

Put meat in shallow dish with next 8 ingredients; mix to coat meat. Heat 2 tablespoons oil in uncovered wok at 350°. Add remaining ingredients; stir-fry 3 to 5 minutes or until vegetables are tender-crisp. Remove from wok; set aside. Wipe out wok with paper towel. Heat remaining 1 tablespoon oil in wok at 400°. Add meat; stir-fry 2 minutes or until no longer pink. Return vegetables to wok; stir-fry to heat through. Serve immediately.

## Tenderloin Stir-Fry

Makes 4 servings
Preparation Time: 15 minutes; 5 minutes to cook

1 **tablespoon cornstarch**
½ **cup cold water**
1 **teaspoon soy sauce**
½ **teaspoon oyster sauce**
1 **tablespoon peanut oil**
1 **pound beef tenderloin,**
**cut in 1-inch cubes**
8 **large fresh mushrooms,**
**wiped clean and sliced**
½ **teaspoon salt**
4 **water chestnuts, sliced**
¼ **pound snow peas, ends**
**and strings removed**
¼ **cup chicken stock**

Mix first 4 ingredients; set aside. Heat oil in uncovered wok at 400°. Add next 3 ingredients; stir-fry 2 minutes. Add remaining ingredients; stir-fry 1 minute. Stir cornstarch mixture; add to wok; stir-fry 1 to 2 minutes. Serve immediately.

Oriental Beef with Vegetables, this page

# Beef

## Stir-Fried Beef and Onions

Makes 2 servings
Preparation Time: 10 minutes; 4 minutes to cook

1 tablespoon cornstarch
2 tablespoons soy sauce
4 tablespoons dry sherry
½ pound lean flank or
   sirloin steak, thinly sliced
   across grain and cut in
   1½-inch-long strips
½ teaspoon sugar
½ teaspoon salt
2 tablespoons peanut oil
2 medium onions, peeled,
   sliced and separated into
   rings

Mix cornstarch, 1 tablespoon soy sauce and 2 tablespoons sherry in bowl. Add meat; stir to coat; set aside to marinate 10 minutes. Stir together remaining soy sauce, remaining sherry, sugar and salt; set aside. Heat oil in uncovered wok at 375°. Add onions; stir-fry 2 minutes. Add beef and soy sauce mixture; stir-fry 2 minutes. Serve immediately.

## Cauliflower and Beef Chinoise

Makes 4 to 6 servings
Preparation Time: 20 minutes; 8 minutes to cook

3 tablespoons peanut oil
1 pound lean flank or
   sirloin steak, thinly sliced
   across grain and cut in
   1½-inch-long strips
1 small onion, peeled,
   halved and thinly sliced
2 cloves garlic, peeled and
   minced
1 cup beef stock
1 small head cauliflower,
   cut into uniform-size
   flowerets
1 cup frozen peas
½ cup fresh bean sprouts
½ cup sliced bamboo
   shoots, drained
1 teaspoon salt
2 tablespoons cornstarch
1 tablespoon soy sauce
½ cup water
2 teaspoons dry sherry

Heat oil in uncovered wok at 375°. Add half of beef; stir-fry 1 minute. Add remaining beef, onion and garlic; stir-fry 1 minute. Add next 6 ingredients; cover; cook until vegetables are barely tender, about 6 minutes. Mix remaining ingredients. Stir; add to wok; stir-fry until sauce thickens slightly. Serve immediately.

## Asparagus and Beef Stir-Fry

Makes 2 servings
Preparation Time: 15 minutes; 6 minutes to cook

- 1 **tablespoon cornstarch**
- ½ **teaspoon sugar**
- 1 **tablespoon cold water**
- 1 **tablespoon hot bean sauce**
- 1 **clove garlic, peeled and crushed**
- 3 **tablespoons peanut oil**
- ½ **pound flank steak, thinly sliced across grain and cut in 1½-inch-long strips**
- 1 **pound asparagus, cut in ½-inch diagonal slices, blanched 2 minutes and drained**
- 1½ **teaspoons salt**

Mix first 3 ingredients; set aside. Mix bean sauce and garlic; set aside. Heat 2 tablespoons oil in uncovered wok at 375°. Add beef; stir-fry 1 minute; remove with strainer. Add remaining 1 tablespoon oil to wok; heat at 375°. Add bean mixture; stir-fry 10 seconds. Add asparagus and salt; stir-fry 1 minute. Return meat to wok; stir cornstarch mixture; add to wok; stir-fry until slightly thickened. Serve immediately.

## Beef Kwangton

Makes 4 servings
Preparation Time: 15 minutes; 5 minutes to cook

- 2 **tablespoons peanut oil**
- 1 **½-inch piece fresh gingerroot, peeled**
- 1 **pound lean flank or sirloin steak, thinly sliced across grain and cut in 1½-inch-long strips**
- ½ **cup sliced bamboo shoots, drained**
- 4 **large fresh mushrooms, wiped clean, thinly sliced**
- 20 **snow peas, ends and strings removed**
- ½ **cup chicken stock**
- 2 **tablespoons oyster sauce**
- ½ **teaspoon soy sauce**
- ¼ **teaspoon sesame oil**
- ¼ **teaspoon sugar**
- ½ **teaspoon salt**
- 1 **tablespoon cornstarch mixed with 1 tablespoon cold water**

Heat oil in uncovered wok at 375°. Swirl gingerroot in oil around wok 30 seconds; discard gingerroot. Add half of beef; stir-fry 1 minute. Add remaining beef; stir-fry 1 minute. Add next 4 ingredients; cover; cook 2 minutes. Meanwhile, mix next 5 ingredients. Uncover; add oyster sauce mixture and cornstarch mixture; stir-fry until sauce thickens. Serve immediately.

# Beef

## Chinese Pepper Steak

Makes 4 servings
Preparation Time: 15 minutes; 5 minutes to cook

1 tablespoon cornstarch
1 cup beef stock
1 tablespoon soy sauce
2 tablespoons peanut oil
1 pound round steak, thinly sliced and cut in 1½-inch-long strips
1 clove garlic, peeled and minced
2 small onions, peeled and each cut into 6 wedges
2 green peppers, cored, seeded and cut into thin 1½-inch-long strips
2 tomatoes, each cut into 8 wedges

1 teaspoon salt
¼ teaspoon freshly ground black pepper
½ teaspoon peeled and minced fresh gingerroot

Mix first 3 ingredients; set aside. Heat oil in uncovered wok at 400°. Add meat and garlic; stir-fry 2 minutes. Add onion, peppers and tomatoes; stir-fry 1 to 2 minutes. Add next 3 ingredients. Stir cornstarch mixture; add to wok; stir-fry until sauce thickens slightly. Serve immediately.

## Curried Beef and Vegetables

Makes 6 servings
Preparation Time: 20 minutes; 7 minutes to cook

¼ teaspoon peeled and minced fresh gingerroot
½ teaspoon sugar
1 tablespoon soy sauce
1 tablespoon curry powder
½ cup beef stock
2 tablespoons peanut oil
1 pound tenderloin, cut in ¼-inch-thick slices, cut across the grain in thin strips
1 medium onion, peeled, quartered and separated into layers
1 medium tomato, cored and cut in 6 wedges
1 green pepper, halved, cored, seeds removed and cut in thin 1½-inch-long strips

2 teaspoons cornstarch mixed with 1 tablespoon cold water

Mix first 5 ingredients; set aside. Heat oil in uncovered wok at 400°. Add meat; stir-fry 1 minute; remove; set aside. Add next 3 ingredients; stir-fry 1 minute. Add curry mixture; cover; cook 2 to 3 minutes. Return meat to wok; stir together. Stir cornstarch mixture; add to wok; stir-fry until slightly thickened. Serve immediately.

Chinese Pepper Steak, this page

# Beef

## Stir-Fried Beef and Pineapple

Makes 4 servings
Preparation Time: 1 hour; 5 minutes to cook

- 2 tablespoons water
- 1 teaspoon baking soda
- 1 pound beef tenderloin, thinly sliced across grain and cut in 1½-inch-long strips
- 1½ tablespoons cornstarch
- 2 tablespoons soy sauce
- ½ teaspoon sesame oil
- 1 tablespoon water
- 2 drops sesame oil
- 1 teaspoon soy sauce
- 2 tablespoons peanut oil
- ½ small red pepper, cored, seeded and cut in thin 1½-inch-long strips
- ½ small green pepper, cored, seeded and cut in thin 1½-inch-long strips
- 2 ¼-inch slices fresh gingerroot, peeled and minced
- 2 small cloves garlic, peeled and minced
- ½ teaspoon sugar
- 1 pineapple, quartered lengthwise through frond, fruit removed and cubed (reserve shells)

Mix water and baking soda; pour over meat; marinate 1 hour. Mix next 3 ingredients; toss with meat. Mix next 3 ingredients; set aside. Heat oil in uncovered wok at 375°. Add next 5 ingredients; stir-fry 1 minute. Add beef and reserved soy sauce mixture; stir-fry 2 minutes. Add cubed pineapple and heat through. Divide among 4 pineapple shells. Serve immediately.

## Beef and Snow Peas

Makes 3 servings
Preparation Time: 15 minutes; 3 minutes to cook

- ¼ cup soy sauce
- 1 tablespoon cornstarch
- 1 tablespoon dry sherry
- 1 teaspoon sugar
- 1 pound flank or sirloin steak, fat trimmed, thinly sliced across grain and cut in 1½-inch-long strips
- 2 tablespoons peanut oil
- ½ teaspoon salt
- 20 snow peas, ends and strings removed
- ½ cup sliced water chestnuts, drained

Mix first 4 ingredients in bowl. Add meat; stir to coat; marinate 15 minutes. Heat oil in uncovered wok at 400°. Add meat; stir-fry 2 minutes. Add salt, snow peas and water chestnuts; stir-fry 1 minute. Serve immediately.

## Hot and Spicy Beef

Makes 4 to 6 servings
Preparation Time: 20 minutes; 5 minutes to cook

1 pound flank steak, thinly sliced across grain and cut in 1½-inch-long strips
1 egg, lightly beaten
1 teaspoon baking soda
3 tablespoons peanut oil
1 tablespoon cornstarch mixed with 1 tablespoon cold water
2 tablespoons peanut oil
1 small red pepper, cored, seeded and cut into thin 1½-inch-long strips
1 small green pepper, cored, seeded and cut into thin 1½-inch-long strips
½ cup sliced water chestnuts, drained
1 tablespoon dry sherry
2 small dried chilies, crushed

1 tablespoon soy sauce
½ teaspoon sugar
½ teaspoon salt
¼ teaspoon sesame oil
1 tablespoon cornstarch mixed with 1 tablespoon cold water

Mix meat with next 4 ingredients in small bowl; set aside to marinate at least 20 minutes. Heat oil in uncovered wok at 400°. Add half of meat mixture; stir-fry 1 minute. Add remaining meat; stir-fry 1 minute. Add next 3 ingredients; stir-fry 1 minute. Add next 6 ingredients; stir-fry 1 minute. Stir cornstarch mixture; add to wok. Stir-fry until sauce thickens. Serve immediately.

## Stir-Fried Round Steak and Vegetables

Makes 4 servings
Preparation Time: 15 minutes; 4 minutes to cook

2 tablespoons peanut oil
1 pound round steak, thinly sliced across grain and cut in 1½-inch-long strips
3 tablespoons soy sauce
1 head bok choy, thinly sliced (Chinese cabbage)
¼ pound fresh mushrooms, sliced
1 8-ounce can sliced water chestnuts, drained
2 teaspoons cornstarch mixed with 2 teaspoons cold water

Heat oil in uncovered wok at 400°. Add half of beef; stir-fry 1 minute. Add remaining beef; stir-fry 1 minute. Add next 4 ingredients; stir-fry 1 minute. Stir cornstarch mixture; add to wok; stir-fry until sauce thickens slightly. Serve immediately.

**Note:** Cook round steak quickly over high heat or it will toughen.

53

# Pork

## Spicy Pork with Vegetables

Makes 2 servings
Preparation Time: 15 minutes; 6 minutes to cook

- 2 tablespoons black bean sauce
- 1 tablespoon soy sauce
- 1 tablespoon dry sherry
- 2 tablespoons peanut oil
- 1 ¼-inch-thick slice fresh gingerroot, peeled and finely minced
- 2 cloves garlic, peeled and minced
- ¼ teaspoon dried red pepper flakes
- 1 large carrot, pared and very thinly sliced on diagonal
- 1 green pepper, cored, seeded and cut in thin 1½-inch-long strips
- ½ pound thinly sliced 1½-inch-long lean pork strips
- ½ cup sliced bamboo shoots, drained
- ½ cup chicken stock
- 2 teaspoons cornstarch mixed with 2 teaspoons cold water

Mix first 3 ingredients; set aside. Heat oil in uncovered wok at 375°. Add next 3 ingredients; stir-fry 30 seconds. Add carrot and green pepper; stir-fry 1 minute. Add pork and bean sauce mixture; stir-fry 2 minutes. Add bamboo shoots and stock; cover; cook 1 minute or until carrots are tender-crisp. Uncover; stir cornstarch mixture; add to wok; stir-fry until sauce thickens. Serve immediately.

## Sliced Pork with Philippine Sauce

Makes 4 servings
Preparation Time: 5 minutes; 15 minutes to cook

- 2 tablespoons peanut oil
- 1 small onion, peeled and finely chopped
- 1 clove garlic, peeled and crushed
- 3 tablespoons packed light brown sugar
- ½ cup lime juice
- ½ cup water
- ½ teaspoon peeled and minced fresh gingerroot
- ½ teaspoon salt
  Dash cayenne pepper
- ½ teaspoon cornstarch mixed with 1 tablespoon cold water
  Hot or cold sliced cooked pork roast

Heat oil in uncovered wok at 350°. Add onion and garlic; stir-fry 1 minute. Add next 6 ingredients; cover; reduce heat to "simmer" for 10 minutes. Stir cornstarch mixture; add to wok and stir. Serve immediately with pork.

Spicy Pork with Vegetables, this page

# Pork

## Oriental Pork and Chinese Cabbage

Makes 4 servings
Preparation Time: 10 minutes; 7 minutes to cook

- 3 tablespoons soy sauce
- 1 tablespoon packed light brown sugar
- 1½ teaspoons salt
- ½ teaspoon peeled and minced fresh gingerroot
- 3 tablespoons peanut oil
- 1 pound 1-inch lean pork cubes
- 1 small green pepper, cored, seeded and cut in thin 1-inch-long strips
- 1 small onion, peeled and cut into wedges
- 4 cups loosely packed shredded Chinese cabbage

- ½ cup cold water
- 1 tablespoon cornstarch mixed with 2 teaspoons cold water

Mix first 4 ingredients; set aside. Heat oil in uncovered wok at 375°. Add pork; stir-fry 3 minutes. Add pepper and onion; stir-fry 1 minute. Add soy sauce mixture, cabbage and water; toss to combine; cover; cook 1 minute. Uncover; stir cornstarch mixture; add to wok; stir-fry until slightly thickened. Serve immediately.

## Mo Shu Pork

Makes 4 servings
Preparation Time: 20 minutes; 4 minutes to cook

- 4 tablespoons peanut oil
- 3 eggs, lightly beaten
- ½ pound pork butt, fat trimmed and cut into thin 1½-inch-long strips
- 1 cup sliced bamboo shoots, drained and thinly sliced into strips
- 10 Chinese dried black mushrooms, soaked in hot water 20 minutes, drained, squeezed dry, stems discarded and caps thinly sliced
- 1 tablespoon soy sauce
- 2 green onions, diagonally cut in ½-inch pieces
- 8 to 10 prepared Chinese Pancakes (Recipe on next page)

Heat 2 tablespoons oil in uncovered wok at 325°. Add eggs; scramble without overcooking. Turn out onto plate. Heat remaining 2 tablespoons oil in wok at 375°. Stir-fry pork 2 minutes. Add bamboo shoots, mushrooms and eggs; stir well, breaking up eggs somewhat. Add soy sauce and green onions; stir-fry 15 seconds. Serve immediately with Chinese Pancakes. Spread some duck sauce on pancakes before filling, if desired. Put a spoonful of pork on a pancake and roll up.

## Chinese Pancakes

Makes 8
Preparation Time: 30 minutes

1 cup flour
½ cup boiling water
2 tablespoons sesame oil

Stir flour and water in bowl until flour comes away from sides of bowl. Knead on lightly floured board until smooth. Cover; let rest 20 minutes. Knead 1 minute; shape into 1½-inch diameter roll. Cut into 8 equal pieces. Flatten each to thin round pancake. Brush 1 side of each pancake with sesame oil; place 2 pancakes together, oiled sides touching. Roll each to 7-inch circle. Heat griddle over medium heat; cook pancake on both sides until slightly puffy. Do not brown. Remove; separate 2 pancakes. Store between sheets of foil; wrap entire stack in foil. Place foil packet on rack or in bamboo steamer in wok. Add hot water to within ½-inch of rack or basket. Bring water to boil at 225°; cover; steam 10 minutes. For extra flavor, spread pancakes with Duck Sauce before filling. Serve with Mo Shu Pork or any shredded meat or vegetable stir-fry.

**Note:** Pancakes can be prepared in advance. Resteam before serving. Pancakes can be frozen. Thaw in foil; steam 20 minutes.

## Pork and Straw Mushroom Stir-Fry

Makes 4 servings
Preparation Time: 30 minutes; 7 minutes to cook

1 tablespoon cornstarch
½ teaspoon salt
½ teaspoon sugar
1 pound lean pork, cut in ½-inch cubes
2 tablespoons soy sauce
1 tablespoon dry sherry
4 tablespoons peanut oil
1 teaspoon peeled and minced fresh gingerroot
2 to 3 thin carrots, pared and sliced diagonally ⅛ inch thick
1 15-ounce can baby ears of corn, drained and rinsed
¼ cup chicken stock
1 15-ounce can straw mushrooms, drained and rinsed
¼ pound snow peas, ends and strings removed

Mix first 3 ingredients in bowl; add meat; toss to coat well. Add soy sauce and wine; toss again; marinate 30 minutes. Heat 2 tablespoons oil in uncovered wok at 400°. Add pork; stir-fry until pinkness is gone; remove with strainer; set aside. Remove oil; wipe wok with paper towel. Heat remaining 2 tablespoons oil in wok at 350°. Add gingerroot and carrots; stir-fry 2 minutes. Add corn; stir-fry 10 seconds. Return pork mixture to wok with stock; stir. Add mushrooms and snow peas; stir-fry 30 seconds. Serve immediately.

## Pork with Green Onions and Water Chestnuts

Makes 4 servings
Preparation Time: 15 minutes; 5 minutes to cook

4 tablespoons soy sauce
2 tablespoons cold water
4 teaspoons cornstarch
1 teaspoon sugar
1½ pounds boneless lean pork, cut in 2 x 2 x ⅛-inch slices
2 tablespoons dry sherry
2 teaspoons rice vinegar
1 teaspoon sesame oil
2 tablespoons peanut oil
2 cloves garlic, peeled and finely minced
4 green onions including tops, cut in ½-inch-long slices
½ cup sliced bamboo shoots, drained

Mix 2 tablespoons soy sauce, cold water, cornstarch and sugar in bowl; add pork; set aside 15 minutes. Mix remaining 2 tablespoons soy sauce, sherry, vinegar and sesame oil; set aside. Heat oil in uncovered wok at 400°. Add garlic; stir-fry 10 seconds. Add pork; stir-fry 3 to 4 minutes. Add onions and bamboo shoots; stir-fry 30 seconds. Add sherry mixture; stir until smooth. Serve immediately.

Sweet and Sour Pork, page 62
Pork and Straw Mushroom Stir-Fry, this page

# Pork

## Stir-Fried Pork with Cashews

Makes 4 servings
Preparation Time: 15 minutes; 6 minutes to cook

2 tablespoons soy sauce
1 tablespoon dry sherry
1 teaspoon salt
   Pinch sugar
2 tablespoons peanut oil
½ teaspoon crushed garlic
3 green onions including
   tops, thinly sliced
1 pound lean boneless
   pork, cut in 1½-inch-long
   thin strips
½ cup sliced bamboo
   shoots, drained
½ cup sliced water
   chestnuts, drained
1 cup fresh bean sprouts
2 teaspoons cornstarch
   mixed with 2 teaspoons
   cold water
⅓ cup unsalted raw cashews

Mix soy sauce, sherry, salt and sugar; set aside. Heat oil in uncovered wok at 350°. Add garlic and onions; stir-fry 1 minute. Add pork; stir-fry until pinkness is gone, about 3 minutes. Add next 3 ingredients and reserved soy sauce mixture; stir-fry 1 minute. Stir cornstarch mixture; add to wok. Stir-fry until sauce thickens. Add cashews; toss to coat. Serve immediately.

## Pork Szechwan

Makes 2 servings
Preparation Time: 15 minutes; 10 minutes to cook

1 cup peanut oil
1 unpeeled small eggplant,
   cut in 2-inch cubes
2 cloves garlic, peeled and
   finely chopped
2 green onions, tops
   discarded, thinly sliced
¼ teaspoon dried red
   pepper flakes
½ pound lean pork butt, cut
   in thin 1½-inch-long
   strips
1 teaspoon dry sherry
2 teaspoons hot bean sauce
½ teaspoon sugar
¼ cup chicken stock
1 tablespoon vinegar
¼ teaspoon sesame oil
1 teaspoon cornstarch
   mixed with 2 tablespoons
   water

Heat oil in uncovered wok at 375°. Add eggplant cubes; fry until golden brown, 4 to 5 minutes. Remove with strainer; drain on paper toweling. Pour all but 1 tablespoon oil from wok. Heat oil in wok at 375°. Add garlic, onions and red pepper flakes; stir-fry 10 seconds. Add pork; stir-fry until it loses its pinkness. Add sherry and eggplant; stir-fry 10 seconds. Add next 5 ingredients; stir-fry 15 seconds. Stir cornstarch mixture; add to wok. Stir-fry until sauce thickens. Serve immediately.

## Pork Strips with Szechwan Sauce

Makes 4 servings
Preparation Time: 15 minutes; 5 minutes to cook

1 **pound lean boneless pork, cut in thin 1½-inch-long strips**
1 **teaspoon minced garlic**
4 **tablespoons soy sauce**
1 **egg, lightly beaten**
2 **tablespoons cornstarch**
1 **tablespoon dry sherry**
2 **tablespoons vinegar**
½ **cup peanut oil**
1 **green pepper, cored, seeded and cut into thin strips**
½ **teaspoon dried red pepper flakes**
4 **green onions including tops, thinly sliced**

Mix pork, ½ teaspoon garlic, 2 tablespoons soy sauce, egg, cornstarch and sherry in bowl; set aside. Mix remaining 2 tablespoons soy sauce and vinegar; set aside. Heat oil in uncovered wok at 400°. Add pork mixture; stir-fry until pork loses its pinkness, 2 to 3 minutes; remove from wok using strainer; set aside. Drain all but 1 tablespoon oil from wok. Heat at 350°. Add green pepper strips, red pepper flakes, remaining ½ teaspoon garlic and onions; stir-fry 30 seconds. Return pork to wok with vinegar mixture; stir-fry 1 minute. Serve immediately.

## Pork Stir-Fry

Makes 4 servings
Preparation Time: 10 minutes; 7 minutes to cook

2 **tablespoons peanut oil**
2 **medium onions, peeled and thinly sliced**
1 **10-inch celery rib, thinly sliced**
2 **cloves garlic, peeled and crushed**
1 **pound thin 1½-inch-long lean pork strips**
¼ **cup chicken stock**
2 **tablespoons dry sherry**
½ **teaspoon salt**
**Freshly ground black pepper to taste**
2 **teaspoons cornstarch mixed with 2 teaspoons cold water**
2 **tablespoons soy sauce**

Heat oil in uncovered wok at 375°. Add onions and celery; stir-fry 2 minutes or until tender-crisp. Add garlic and pork; stir-fry until pork loses its pinkness, 2 to 3 minutes. Add next 4 ingredients; stir-fry 30 seconds. Stir cornstarch mixture; add to wok with soy sauce; stir-fry until sauce thickens. Serve immediately.

# Pork

## Sweet and Sour Pork

Makes 6 servings
Preparation Time: 20 minutes; 15 minutes to cook

2 **pounds boneless pork
loin, cut in ½-inch cubes**
¼ **cup soy sauce**
1 **egg, lightly beaten
Cornstarch, about 1 cup**
1½ **cups vegetable oil**
1 **large onion, peeled and
cut in 8 wedges**
1 **green pepper, cored,
seeded and cut in 1-inch
pieces**
1 **cup pineapple chunks,
drained and juice
reserved**
2 **small tomatoes, cored
and cut in wedges
Sweet and Sour Sauce**

Toss pork with soy sauce; roll in egg; roll in cornstarch, shaking off excess cornstarch. Heat oil in uncovered wok at 400°. Add pork in 4 batches, stir-frying until golden brown. Drain on paper towels; keep warm in preheated 200° oven. Drain all but 1 tablespoon oil from wok; heat at 350°. Add onion; stir-fry 2 minutes. Add green pepper; stir-fry 2 minutes. Add pineapple and tomatoes; stir-fry 1 minute. Return pork to wok; add Sweet and Sour Sauce; stir-fry to coat with sauce. Serve immediately.

## Sweet and Sour Sauce

½ **cup reserved pineapple
juice**
½ **cup white wine vinegar**
2 **tablespoons peanut oil**
2 **tablespoons packed light
brown sugar**
1 **tablespoon soy sauce**
½ **teaspoon freshly ground
black pepper**
2 **teaspoons cornstarch
mixed with 4 teaspoons
cold water**

Mix first 6 ingredients in wok; bring to boil at 225°. Stir cornstarch mixture; add to wok, stirring until sauce is clear and slightly thickened. Sauce may also be prepared in saucepan.

# Chicken

## Almond Chicken

Makes 4 servings
Preparation Time: 15 minutes; 7 minutes to cook

**2 tablespoons peanut oil**
**1 whole chicken breast, split, skinned, boned and thinly sliced**
**½ cup sliced bamboo shoots, drained**
**½ teaspoon salt**
**½ cup sliced water chestnuts, drained**
**½ cup slivered almonds**
**2 tablespoons soy sauce**
**1 cup chicken stock**
**3 tablespoons cornstarch mixed with ½ cup cold water**

Heat oil in uncovered wok at 375°. Add chicken; stir-fry 3 minutes or until chicken is opaque. Add next 6 ingredients; cover; cook 3 minutes. Stir cornstarch mixture; add to wok. Stir-fry until slightly thickened. Serve immediately.

## Stir-Fried Chicken and Vegetables

Makes 4 servings
Preparation Time: 15 minutes; 5 minutes to cook

**½ cup cold water**
**2 teaspoons cornstarch**
**½ teaspoon peeled and finely minced fresh gingerroot**
**2 teaspoons soy sauce**
**2 tablespoons peanut oil**
**1 medium onion, peeled, halved and sliced**
**1 teaspoon minced garlic**
**1 whole chicken breast, split, skinned, boned and cut in ¾-inch pieces**
**1 green pepper, cored, seeded and cut in thin 1½-inch-long strips**
**2 tomatoes, cored and each cut in 6 wedges**

Mix water, cornstarch, gingerroot and soy sauce; set aside. Heat oil in uncovered wok at 375°. Add onion and garlic; stir-fry 1 minute. Add chicken and green pepper; stir-fry 3 minutes. Add tomatoes; stir-fry 1 minute. Stir cornstarch mixture; add to wok; cook until sauce thickens. Serve immediately.

# Chicken

## Chicken with Hoisin Sauce and Nuts

Makes 4 servings
Preparation Time: 20 minutes; 7 minutes to cook

- 1 **tablespoon cornstarch**
- 2 **tablespoons dry sherry**
- 2 **whole chicken breasts, split, skinned, boned and cut into 1-inch cubes**
- 3 **tablespoons peanut oil**
- 6 **large Chinese dried black mushrooms, soaked in hot water 20 minutes, drained, stems discarded, caps quartered**
- 1 **small green pepper, cored, seeded and cut in thin 1½-inch-long strips**
- ½ **cup sliced water chestnuts, drained**
- ½ **teaspoon salt**
- 1 **tablespoon sugar mixed with 3 tablespoons hoisin sauce**
- ¼ **cup unsalted raw cashews, almonds, pecans** or **peanuts**

Mix cornstarch and sherry in bowl; add chicken; stir; set aside. Heat 1 tablespoon oil in uncovered wok at 375°; add mushrooms; stir-fry 1 minute. Add pepper and water chestnuts; stir-fry 1 minute. Add salt; mix. Remove vegetables from wok with strainer; set aside. Add remaining 2 tablespoons oil to wok; heat at 375°. Add chicken; stir-fry 3 minutes or until opaque. Add sugar-hoisin mixture; toss well. Return vegetables to wok; mix. Add nuts; mix. Serve immediately.

## Chicken Livers Chinese-Style

Makes 4 servings
Preparation Time: 10 minutes; 10 minutes to cook

- 2 **tablespoons soy sauce**
- 2 **tablespoons water**
- 1 **tablespoon cornstarch**
- 3 **slices bacon**
- 1 **pound chicken livers, fat trimmed, each cut in 3 pieces**
- 4 **green onions including tops, chopped**
- 1 **medium green pepper, cored, seeded and chopped**

Mix first 3 ingredients; set aside. Fry bacon in wok at 325° until crisp; drain; crumble; set aside. Brown livers and onions in fat in wok, about 3 minutes. Near end of browning, add green pepper. Stir soy mixture; add to wok. Stir until sauce thickens slightly. Stir in reserved bacon. Serve immediately.

## Lemon Chicken

Makes 2 to 4 servings
Preparation Time: 40 minutes

1 **chicken**
**Chicken stock**
**Juice of 3 lemons**
½ **cup sugar**
½ **cup boiling water**

Simmer chicken in chicken stock to cover in wok at 225° until nearly tender, about 20 minutes. Remove; halve lengthwise; place on broiler rack. Broil 4 to 5 inches from heat 10 minutes; turn; broil another 10 minutes or until golden brown. Meanwhile, mix lemon juice, sugar and boiling water in saucepan. Bring to boil; simmer 2 to 3 minutes. Remove from heat; set aside. Arrange chicken halves on platter; spoon lemon sauce over chicken.

## Shredded Chicken Hunan-Style

Makes 4 servings
Preparation Time: 15 minutes; 3 to 4 minutes to cook

⅓ **cup dry sherry**
¼ **teaspoon salt**
¼ **teaspoon sugar**
¼ **cup chicken stock**
4 **green onions including tops, cut in ½-inch pieces**
2 **¼-inch slices fresh gingerroot, peeled and diced**
1 **tablespoon cornstarch mixed with 2 tablespoons cold water**
1 **whole chicken breast, split, skinned, boned and cut in ⅛-inch-thick slices**
2 **egg whites**
½ **teaspoon salt**
2 **tablespoons dry sherry**
3 **tablespoons cornstarch**
1½ **cups peanut oil**
12 **snow peas, ends and strings removed**
2 **cups fresh bean sprouts**

Mix ⅓ cup dry sherry and next 6 ingredients; set aside. Put chicken shreds in bowl with next 3 ingredients; mix with fork vigorously until chicken is coated. Add cornstarch; mix with fork until smooth. Heat oil in uncovered wok at 300°. Add chicken mixture; stir-fry 1 minute, breaking up chicken with spatula. Remove chicken with strainer; pour all but 1 tablespoon oil from wok; heat oil in wok at 350°. Add snow peas and bean sprouts; stir-fry 15 seconds. Return chicken to wok; add sherry mixture; cook until sauce is thickened. Serve immediately.

**Note:** Slicing chicken is easier when chicken is partially frozen.

65

# Chicken

## Chicken with Cashews and Snow Peas

Makes 2 servings
Preparation Time: 15 minutes; 5 minutes to cook

- 1 **whole chicken breast, split, skinned, boned and cut in 1-inch cubes**
- 2 **cloves garlic, peeled and minced**
- 1 **tablespoon soy sauce**
- 1 **tablespoon dry sherry**
- 2 **tablespoons cornstarch**
- 1 **teaspoon hoisin sauce**
- 1 **tablespoon peanut oil**
- 20 **snow peas, ends and strings removed**
- ½ **cup sliced water chestnuts, drained**
- ½ **cup hot chicken stock**
- ½ **teaspoon salt**
- ½ **cup unsalted raw cashews**

Marinate chicken 15 minutes in mixture of next 5 ingredients. Heat oil in uncovered wok at 375°. Add chicken mixture; stir-fry 3 minutes. Add snow peas and water chestnuts; stir-fry 30 seconds. Add stock and salt; stir-fry until slightly thickened. Stir in cashews. Serve immediately.

## Chicken with Oyster Sauce

Makes 4 servings
Preparation Time: 15 minutes; 6 minutes to cook

- 1 **tablespoon soy sauce**
- ½ **teaspoon sugar**
- ½ **teaspoon salt**
- 1 **tablespoon oyster sauce**
- 2 **tablespoons peanut oil**
- 1 **clove garlic, peeled and split**
- 1 **large green pepper, cored, seeded and cut in 1-inch pieces**
- 1 **onion, peeled and cut in 1-inch cubes**
- 2 **whole chicken breasts, split, skinned, boned and cut in 1-inch cubes**

Mix soy sauce, sugar, salt and oyster sauce; set aside. Heat oil in uncovered wok at 375°. Swirl garlic around sides and bottom of wok about 30 seconds; discard. Add pepper and onion; stir-fry 1 minute. Add chicken; stir-fry 3 minutes or until opaque. Add soy sauce mixture; stir well. Serve immediately.

Chicken with Cashews and Snow Peas, this page

# Chicken

## Chicken with Button Mushrooms

Makes 2 servings
Preparation Time: 10 minutes; 7 minutes to cook

1 teaspoon cornstarch
mixed with 1 teaspoon
cold water
1 tablespoon dry sherry
1 tablespoon oyster sauce
1 teaspoon water
½ teaspoon salt
1 whole chicken breast,
split, skinned, boned and
cubed
2 teaspoons dry white wine
or dry vermouth
1 egg white, lightly beaten
1 teaspoon cornstarch
Salt and freshly ground
white pepper to taste
2 tablespoons peanut oil
¼ pound snow peas, ends
and strings removed
¼ cup sliced water
chestnuts, drained
¼ cup sliced bamboo
shoots, drained
24 fresh button mushrooms

Stir cornstarch mixture; add next 4 ingredients; mix well; set aside. Mix next 4 ingredients; season with salt and pepper. Heat oil in uncovered wok at 375°. Add chicken; stir-fry until opaque. Add snow peas, water chestnuts, bamboo shoots and mushrooms; stir-fry 3 minutes. Stir sherry mixture; add to wok. Cook, stirring, 1 minute. Serve immediately.

## Szechwan Chicken

Makes 4 servings
Preparation Time: 15 minutes; 6 minutes to cook

1 tablespoon cornstarch
3 tablespoons soy sauce
2 whole chicken breasts,
split, skinned, boned and
cut in ½-inch cubes
1 tablespoon dry sherry
2 teaspoons sugar
1 teaspoon vinegar
¼ cup peanut oil
½ to 1 teaspoon dried red
pepper flakes
2 green onions including
tops, sliced
½ teaspoon peeled and
minced fresh gingerroot
½ cup dry-roasted peanuts
Hot cooked rice

Blend cornstarch and 1 tablespoon soy sauce in bowl. Mix in chicken; set aside. Mix remaining 2 tablespoons soy sauce, sherry, sugar and vinegar; set aside. Heat oil in uncovered wok at 375°. When hot, add red pepper flakes; stir-fry until black, 10 seconds. Add chicken; stir-fry 2 minutes. Remove chicken with strainer; set aside. Add green onions and gingerroot; stir-fry 1 minute. Add chicken; stir-fry 2 minutes. Add sherry mixture; stir-fry 1 minute. Stir in peanuts. Serve with hot rice.

## Walnut Chicken

Makes 4 servings
Preparation Time: 20 minutes; 8 minutes to cook

- ½ cup water
- 2 tablespoons cornstarch
- 1 tablespoon soy sauce
- ½ teaspoon sugar
- ½ teaspoon salt
- 3 tablespoons peanut oil
- 1 cup walnut halves
- 1 whole chicken breast, split, skinned, boned and slivered
- 6 Chinese dried black mushrooms, soaked in hot water 20 minutes, drained, stems discarded, caps quartered
- 12 snow peas, ends and strings removed
- 6 fresh mushrooms, wiped clean and sliced
- ½ cup sliced water chestnuts, drained
- ½ cup sliced bamboo shoots, drained

Mix first 5 ingredients; set aside. Heat 1 tablespoon oil in uncovered wok at 300°; add walnuts; stir-fry 1 minute. Do not let burn. Remove walnuts with strainer; drain on paper towel. Discard oil in wok. Heat remaining 2 tablespoons oil in wok at 375°. Add chicken; stir-fry 3 minutes. Add next 5 ingredients; stir-fry 3 minutes. Add cornstarch mixture; cook until thickened. Serve immediately topped with walnuts.

## Chicken Delicious

Makes 4 servings
Preparation Time: 20 minutes; 4 minutes to cook

- 2 whole chicken breasts, split, skinned, boned and cut in 1-inch cubes
- 1 tablespoon cornstarch
- 1 tablespoon dry sherry
- 1 tablespoon soy sauce
- 2 tablespoons peanut oil
- ¼ pound fresh mushrooms, wiped clean and sliced
- 1 green pepper, cored, seeded and cut in 1-inch pieces
- 1 heaping tablespoon hoisin sauce
  Salt to taste
- ⅓ cup unsalted raw cashews

Sprinkle chicken with cornstarch; toss to coat thoroughly. Add sherry and soy sauce; marinate 15 minutes at room temperature. Heat oil in uncovered wok at 375°. Add chicken; stir-fry 3 minutes. Add mushrooms and green pepper; stir-fry 45 seconds. Add remaining ingredients; toss to mix. Serve immediately.

# Chicken

## Chinese Chicken and Shrimp Salad

Makes 6 servings
Preparation Time: 20 minutes

- 2 **cups peanut oil**
- 6 **ounces rice sticks**
- 2 **whole chicken breasts, cooked, skinned, boned and shredded**
- ½ **pound medium shrimp, shelled, deveined and cooked**
- 1 **cup thinly sliced celery**
- 1 **cup slivered almonds**
- 1 **large zucchini, cut in 2-inch-long julienne strips**
- 1 **head iceberg lettuce, shredded**
- 1 **cup thinly sliced red radishes**
- 1 **cup chopped green onions**
   **Dressing**

Heat 2 cups oil in uncovered wok at 375°. Drop rice sticks, 1 ounce at a time, into oil. After they puff (about 30 seconds), remove immediately. Do not brown. Drain on paper towels. Cool; store in airtight container until serving time. To serve, toss rice sticks, chicken, shrimp, celery, almonds and zucchini in bowl. Toss remaining ingredients except Dressing in large bowl; top with ingredients in other bowl; toss. Add desired amount of Dressing; toss. Serve immediately.

## Dressing

Makes approximately 1¼ cups.

- 2 **tablespoons sesame oil**
- ¼ **cup peanut oil**
- ½ **cup cider vinegar**
- ¼ **cup soy sauce**
- ½ **teaspoon sugar**
- 1 **teaspoon five-spice powder**
- 1 **clove garlic, peeled and minced**
- 2 **tablespoons toasted sesame seed**

Place all ingredients in jar with tight-fitting lid; let stand at room temperature at least 1 hour to blend flavors. Shake before serving.

## Crisp Chicken Salad

Makes 4 servings
Preparation Time: 20 minutes; 3 hours to marinate

**2 whole chicken breasts, split, skinned and boned**
**1½ cups chicken stock**
**½ cup sliced green onions**
**½ cup sliced water chestnuts, drained**
**¼ cup sesame seed, lightly toasted**
**¼ pound snow peas, ends and strings removed, cut in julienne strips**
**Dressing**
**Salt and freshly ground black pepper to taste**

Simmer chicken breasts in chicken stock at 225° for 15 minutes. Let cool in broth; remove; cut meat in ¼-inch strips. Mix chicken, green onions, water chestnuts, sesame seed and snow peas in large bowl. Toss with enough Dressing to coat ingredients. Season with salt and pepper. Serve immediately.

## Dressing

Makes 1 cup

**1 ¼-inch slice fresh gingerroot, peeled**
**2 tablespoons dry sherry**
**1 egg yolk**
**1 tablespoon Dijon mustard**
**1½ teaspoons fresh lemon juice**
**½ cup peanut oil or ¼ cup peanut oil and ¼ cup olive oil**
**1 tablespoon soy sauce**
**Salt and freshly ground white pepper to taste**

Marinate gingerroot in sherry 3 hours. Beat yolk with mustard. Add lemon juice; beat to combine. Add oil in thin stream, whisking constantly until thickened and smooth. Remove gingerroot from sherry; add soy sauce, whisking constantly. Season with salt and pepper.

# Chicken

## Eight Delicious Chicken

Makes 4 servings
Preparation Time: 20 minutes; 10 minutes to cook

1½ cups peanut or vegetable oil
1 whole chicken breast, split, skinned, boned and cut into ½-inch cubes
½ cup small shelled shrimp
1 tablespoon peeled and diced fresh gingerroot
1 clove garlic, peeled and finely chopped
¼ cup sliced bamboo shoots, drained
¼ cup sliced water chestnuts, drained
6 canned Chinese baby corn, drained
½ cup button mushrooms
8 to 10 Chinese dried black mushrooms, soaked in hot water 20 minutes, drained, stems discarded, caps quartered
2 tablespoons dry sherry

1 tablespoon sugar
3 tablespoons soy sauce
2 teaspoons hoisin sauce
½ cup unsalted peanuts

Heat oil in wok at 325°. Add chicken; stir-fry 3 minutes. Add shrimp; stir-fry until pink. Remove chicken and shrimp with strainer; set aside. Drain all but 2 tablespoons oil from wok. (Oil can be reserved for future use.) Increase heat to 375°; add gingerroot and garlic; stir-fry 10 seconds. Add bamboo shoots, water chestnuts, baby corn, button and black mushrooms; stir-fry until vegetables are tender-crisp, about 3 minutes. Mix sherry, sugar, soy and hoisin sauce; pour over vegetables. Add chicken and shrimp; stir-fry 2 minutes. Add peanuts; stir. Serve immediately.

## Steamed Chicken with Vegetables

Makes 4 servings
Preparation Time: 20 minutes; 45 minutes to cook

1 chicken, cut into serving pieces
2 unpeeled zucchini, cut in thick diagonal slices
2 large carrots, pared and cut in thick diagonal slices
2 potatoes, peeled and sliced diagonally
1 large rib celery, sliced diagonally
2 sprigs parsley
½ teaspoon dried tarragon

1 bay leaf
Salt to taste
Sauce (Recipe on next page)

Place chicken pieces on steamer rack in wok. Top with next 7 ingredients. Season with salt. Cover; steam at 225° over hot water 45 minutes or until chicken and vegetables are tender. Add more water if necessary. Remove bay leaf. Serve with Sauce.

## Sauce

Makes approximately 1 cup

1 **cup dry white wine** or **dry vermouth**
1 **shallot, peeled and minced**
1 **tablespoon unsalted butter**
1 **cup chicken stock**
   **Freshly ground white pepper to taste**

Boil wine in wok at 225° until reduced by half. In another wok or saucepan, sauté shallot in butter 4 to 5 minutes at 325° or medium-low heat. Do not brown. Add to wok with stock; cook until reduced by one-third. Season with pepper.

## Spiced Orange Chicken

Makes 4 servings
Preparation Time: 15 minutes; 6 to 7 minutes to cook

2 **whole chicken breasts, split, skinned, boned and cut in 1-inch cubes**
1 **teaspoon salt**
1 **egg, lightly beaten**
2 **tablespoons cornstarch**
5 **tablespoons peanut oil, divided**
2 **tablespoons soy sauce**
1 **tablespoon sugar**
1 **teaspoon sesame oil**
1 **tablespoon dry sherry**
1 **teaspoon white vinegar**
   **Grated peel from 2 tangerines**
¼ **teaspoon dried red pepper flakes**
4 **¼-inch slices fresh gingerroot, peeled and coarsely chopped**
3 **to 4 green onions, cut diagonally in ¼-inch slices**

Mix chicken, salt, egg, 1 tablespoon cornstarch and 1 tablespoon oil in bowl until chicken is coated; set aside. Mix next 5 ingredients and remaining 1 tablespoon cornstarch; set aside. Heat 3 tablespoons oil in uncovered wok at 375°. Stir-fry chicken until opaque, about 3 minutes. Remove with strainer; set aside. Heat 1 tablespoon oil in wok at 350°; add tangerine peel and red pepper flakes. Cook until blackened, about 10 seconds, stirring constantly. Add gingerroot, green onions and chicken; stir-fry 10 seconds. Stir soy mixture; add to wok; stir-fry 1 minute. Serve immediately.

# Fish and Seafood

## Steamed Fish Chinois

Makes 4 servings
Preparation Time: 1 hour; 10 to 15 minutes to cook

3 tablespoons soy sauce
½ cup dry sherry
2 tablespoons fresh lemon juice
1 clove garlic, peeled and crushed
2 pounds halibut, salmon, haddock or cod fillets
2 to 3 cups water

Mix first 4 ingredients in shallow baking dish. Add fillets; marinate 1 hour. Heat water in wok at 225° until simmering. Place fillets in steamer basket or on steamer ring in 1 layer over simmering water. Cover; steam fish until opaque, 10 minutes per 1-inch thickness of fish. Serve immediately.

## Jade Fish

Makes 4 servings
Preparation Time: 15 minutes; 20 minutes to cook

1 2-pound bass or red snapper, cleaned, head and tail intact or 1-inch-thick fillets
2 to 3 cups hot water
Lettuce leaves
¼ cup peanut oil
20 snow peas, ends and strings removed
½ pound sliced fresh mushrooms
1½ cups fish stock
5 green onions including tops, cut in 1½-inch diagonal slices
2 teaspoons soy sauce
1 tablespoon oyster sauce
¼ teaspoon dried red pepper flakes, optional
1 teaspoon vinegar
½ teaspoon salt
½ teaspoon sugar

2 tablespoons cornstarch mixed with ¼ cup cold water

Put fish on rack in wok or in steamer basket. Add hot water; cover; steam at 225° for 10 to 15 minutes or until fish is opaque. Meanwhile, line deep platter with lettuce leaves. Carefully lift fish from water using slotted spatula; place on lettuce. Clean wok. Heat oil in uncovered wok at 375°. Add snow peas; stir-fry 30 seconds; remove with strainer; set aside. Add mushrooms; stir-fry 1 minute. Add next 8 ingredients; bring to boil. Stir cornstarch mixture; add to wok; stir until slightly thickened. Add snow peas; reheat. Arrange snow peas around fish; pour sauce over all. Serve immediately.

Jade Fish, this page

# Fish and Seafood

## Steamed Bass

Makes 4 servings
Preparation Time: 10 minutes; 20 minutes to cook

- 1 **sea bass** or **striped bass (about 3 pounds cleaned) with head and tail intact**
- 1 **tablespoon salt**
  **Water**
- 1 **tablespoon peanut oil**
- 2 **¼-inch slices fresh gingerroot, peeled and minced**
- 4 **small cloves garlic, peeled and crushed**
- 3 **green onions including tops, cut in 1-inch pieces**
- 2 **tablespoons dry sherry**
- ¼ **cup soy sauce**
- 1 **teaspoon sesame oil**

Rinse and pat fish dry; sprinkle with salt. Place fish on heatproof plate. Place plate on rack inside wok, or place fish in steamer basket. Add enough water to wok around plate or steamer basket to come within ½ inch of plate or basket. Bring water to boil at 225°. Meanwhile, heat oil in another wok or skillet at 350°. Add next 4 ingredients; stir-fry 30 seconds. Add remaining ingredients; stir. Pour over fish; cover wok or put top on steamer basket. Let water boil 15 minutes or until fish is steamed to desired doneness. Serve immediately.

## Walnut Shrimp

Makes 4 servings
Preparation Time: 10 minutes; 7 minutes to cook

- 1 **pound medium shrimp, shelled, deveined, cut in thirds**
- 2 **teaspoons soy sauce**
- 2 **teaspoons dry sherry**
- ¼ **teaspoon freshly ground white pepper**
- 1 **teaspoon cornstarch**
- 3 **tablespoons peanut oil**
- ½ **cup sliced bamboo shoots, drained**
- ½ **cup walnuts**
- 1 **¼-inch slice fresh gingerroot, peeled**
- 2 **green onions including tops, sliced diagonally in 1-inch pieces**
- 1 **teaspoon salt**
- ½ **teaspoon sesame oil**

Toss first 5 ingredients and 1 tablespoon oil in bowl; set aside. Heat 1 tablespoon oil in uncovered wok at 350°. Add bamboo shoots and walnuts; stir-fry 1 minute; set aside. Wipe out wok with paper towels. Heat remaining 1 tablespoon oil in wok at 375°. Swirl gingerroot slice around wok 30 seconds; discard. Add onions and shrimp mixture; stir-fry 2 minutes. Add bamboo shoots and walnuts; stir to combine. Add salt and sesame oil; stir to combine. Serve immediately.

# Fish and Seafood

## Crab Stir-Fry with Cashews

Makes 4 servings
Preparation Time: 15 minutes; 5 minutes to cook

1 tablespoon cornstarch
1 tablespoon soy sauce
1 tablespoon fresh lemon juice
¾ cup chicken stock
2 tablespoons peanut oil
¼ pound fresh mushrooms, wiped clean and thinly sliced
1 6-ounce can crab meat, drained
4 green onions including tops, cut in thin diagonal slices
¼ cup sliced water chestnuts, drained
20 snow peas, ends and strings removed
⅓ cup unsalted cashews

Mix first 4 ingredients; set aside. Heat oil in uncovered wok at 375°. Add mushrooms; stir-fry 1 minute. Add next 3 ingredients; stir-fry 1 minute. Add snow peas; stir-fry 1 minute. Stir cornstarch mixture; add to wok; stir-fry until slightly thickened. Add nuts; toss to combine. Serve immediately.

## Fish and Snow Peas

Makes 4 servings
Preparation Time: 15 minutes; 4 minutes to cook

1 pound cod fillets, cut in 1 x 3 x ½-inch pieces
2 tablespoons cornstarch
1 egg white, lightly beaten
1 clove garlic, peeled and crushed
1 green onion, thinly sliced
½ cup sliced water chestnuts, drained
20 to 30 snow peas, ends and strings removed
¼ cup dry sherry
1 teaspoon sugar
½ teaspoon salt
½ teaspoon sesame oil
1 tablespoon cold water
2 tablespoons peanut oil

Toss fish, 1 tablespoon cornstarch and egg white in bowl; set aside. Combine garlic and onion; set aside. Combine water chestnuts and snow peas; set aside. Mix next 5 ingredients with remaining 1 tablespoon cornstarch; set aside. Heat 1 tablespoon oil in uncovered wok at 350°. Add garlic mixture; stir-fry 15 seconds. Add snow pea mixture; stir-fry 30 seconds; remove from wok using strainer; set aside. Heat remaining 1 tablespoon oil in wok until hot. Add fish; gently stir-fry 1 minute. Return vegetables to wok; stir-fry 15 seconds. Stir cornstarch mixture; add to wok. Stir gently until sauce thickens slightly. Serve immediately.

# Fish and Seafood

## Sweet and Sour Salmon

Makes 4 servings
Preparation Time: 15 minutes; 40 minutes to cook

1½ cups water
1 carrot, pared and thinly sliced
1 tablespoon peanut oil
1 onion, peeled and thinly sliced
1 teaspoon fresh lemon juice
2 tablespoons sugar
½ cup vinegar
10 whole peppercorns
2 ribs celery, cut in 4-inch pieces
3 whole cloves
2 pounds salmon steaks, each 1-inch thick
⅓ to ½ cup vinegar
10 gingersnaps, crumbled
¾ cup packed light brown sugar
¼ cup seedless raisins
¼ cup dry sherry
¼ cup slivered almonds

Mix first 7 ingredients in wok. Tie peppercorns, celery and cloves in cheesecloth bag; add to wok. Bring to boil at 225°; reduce heat to "simmer" for 20 minutes. Add salmon steaks; poach gently 10 minutes. Remove steaks with slotted spatula to warm serving platter; keep warm. Remove cheesecloth bag from wok. Pour enough vinegar over gingersnap crumbs to dissolve them. Add to liquid in wok with next 3 ingredients; boil 4 minutes at 225°. Add almonds; pour over fish. Serve immediately.

## Shrimp Egg Foo Yung

Makes 4 servings
Preparation Time: 5 minutes; 20 to 30 minutes to cook

1 cup fresh bean sprouts
½ cup sliced water chestnuts, drained and chopped
1 6¼-ounce can small shrimp, drained
4 eggs, lightly beaten
1 teaspoon salt
½ teaspoon freshly ground white pepper
3 tablespoons peanut oil
Sauce

Mix all ingredients except oil and Sauce in bowl. Heat 1 tablespoon oil in uncovered wok at 325°. Pour ¼ of mixture into wok; form into round cake; brown on both sides about 2 to 3 minutes per side. Remove; keep warm. Brown remaining cakes using remaining oil as needed. Serve immediately with Sauce.

# Fish and Seafood

## Sauce

1½ teaspoons packed light brown sugar
¼ cup boiling beef stock
1 tablespoon cornstarch mixed with 2 tablespoons cold water
1 tablespoon soy sauce
1 tablespoon dark molasses
Pinch freshly ground black pepper

Dissolve brown sugar in beef stock in saucepan. Stir cornstarch mixture; add to saucepan with remaining ingredients; stir over medium heat until thickened.

## Sweet and Sour Shrimp

Makes 4 servings
Preparation Time: 15 minutes; 9 minutes to cook

½ cup flour
2 tablespoons cornstarch
½ teaspoon baking powder
½ teaspoon salt
1 egg
1½ cups water
1 cup peanut oil plus 2 teaspoons
16 large shrimp, shelled except for tail portion, deveined
½ cup catsup
2 tablespoons white vinegar
3 tablespoons sugar
1 large green pepper, cored, seeded and cut in 1-inch chunks
1 large onion, peeled, cut in eighths, separated into pieces
1 15½-ounce can pineapple chunks, drained
2 teaspoons cornstarch mixed with 2 teaspoons cold water

Mix flour, cornstarch, baking powder, salt, egg, ½ cup water and 1 teaspoon oil in bowl until smooth; set aside. Heat 1 cup oil in uncovered wok at 375°. Holding shrimp by tail, dip one at a time into batter, letting excess drip back into bowl. Slide shrimp into hot oil; fry until golden brown, 1 to 2 minutes each. Fry two or three at a time. Drain on paper towels. Pour out all oil except 1 tablespoon. Add remaining 1 cup water, 1 teaspoon oil, catsup, vinegar and sugar to wok; bring to boil at 250°. Add green pepper and onion; return to boil. Stir-fry 2 minutes. Add pineapple; return to boil. Stir cornstarch mixture; add to wok; stir to thicken. Add shrimp; stir gently until heated through. Serve immediately.

# Fish and Seafood

## Stir-Fried Shrimp

Makes 4 servings
Preparation Time: 25 minutes; 4½ minutes to cook

2 ¼-inch slices fresh
   gingerroot, peeled
1 large clove garlic, peeled
2 tablespoons soy sauce
1 tablespoon dry sherry
2 tablespoons catsup
1 teaspoon sugar
   Pinch cayenne pepper
2 tablespoons peanut oil
1 pound raw shrimp,
   shelled, deveined and
   patted dry
2 green onions including
   tops, cut diagonally into
   1-inch pieces

Crush gingerroot and garlic together; set aside. Mix next 5 ingredients; set aside. Heat oil in uncovered wok at 375°. Add gingerroot and garlic; stir-fry 10 seconds. Add shrimp; stir-fry 3 minutes or until pink. Add green onion; stir-fry 30 seconds. Add soy sauce mixture; stir-fry 30 seconds. Serve immediately.

**Note:** For hotter taste, use ⅛ teaspoon cayenne pepper.

## Spicy Shrimp

Makes 3 servings
Preparation Time: 10 minutes; 3 minutes to cook

½ teaspoon soy sauce
½ teaspoon sugar
½ teaspoon ground
   coriander
½ cup chicken stock
1 pound shrimp, shelled
   and deveined
1 teaspoon dry sherry
1 egg white, lightly beaten
1½ teaspoons cornstarch
2 tablespoons peanut oil
½ teaspoon dried red
   pepper flakes
½ cup thin diagonal celery
   slices
8 Chinese dried black
   mushrooms, soaked in ½
   cup hot water 20
   minutes, drained, stems
   discarded, caps cut in
   thin strips

1 teaspoon cornstarch
   mixed with 1 teaspoon
   cold water

Mix first 4 ingredients; set aside. Put next 4 ingredients in bowl; toss to coat. Heat oil in uncovered wok at 375°; add pepper; stir-fry 30 seconds. Add shrimp; stir-fry 1 minute. Add celery and mushrooms; stir-fry 1 minute. Add soy sauce mixture; stir-fry 30 seconds. Add cornstarch mixture; stir until slightly thickened. Serve immediately.

# Fish and Seafood

## Shrimp in Bean Sauce

Makes 4 servings
Preparation Time: 15 minutes; 6 minutes to cook

1 tablespoon dry sherry
2 teaspoons peeled and minced fresh gingerroot
1 tablespoon soy sauce
¼ teaspoon freshly ground white pepper
1 pound large shrimp, shelled except for tail, deveined
4 tablespoons peanut oil
1 small onion, peeled, halved and sliced
1 cup frozen tiny peas
½ small green pepper, cored, seeded and cut in ½-inch-long strips
½ small red pepper, cored, seeded and cut in ½-inch-long strips
2 cloves garlic, peeled and minced
2 tablespoons bean sauce
2 teaspoons cornstarch mixed with 2 tablespoons cold water

Mix first 4 ingredients; pour over shrimp; marinate 15 minutes; drain. Heat 2 tablespoons oil in uncovered wok at 375°. Stir-fry next 4 ingredients 2 minutes; remove with strainer; set aside. Add remaining 2 tablespoons oil; stir-fry garlic and bean sauce 10 seconds. Add shrimp; stir-fry until pink, about 2 minutes. Return vegetables to wok; stir cornstarch mixture; add to wok. Stir-fry until sauce thickens. Serve immediately.

## Poor Man's Lobster

Makes 6 servings
Preparation Time: 20 minutes

2 pounds cod fillets
Water
1 teaspoon salt
1 bay leaf
1 small onion, peeled and sliced
1 slice lemon
½ cup dry vermouth
Hot melted butter
Chopped fresh parsley

Place fish in wok. Cover with water and next 5 ingredients; bring to boil at 225°. Reduce heat to "simmer" for 8 to 10 minutes or until fish is opaque. Carefully remove fish from wok with slotted spatula. Serve hot with melted butter and chopped parsley.

# Fish and Seafood

## Oriental Scallops

Makes 6 servings
Preparation Time: 10 minutes; 5 minutes to cook

¼ cup cold water
2 tablespoons cornstarch
1 tablespoon soy sauce
½ teaspoon salt
⅛ teaspoon freshly ground white pepper
2 tablespoons peanut oil
2 pounds scallops, halved if large
30 snow peas, ends and strings removed
2 medium tomatoes, cored and each cut into 6 wedges

Mix first 5 ingredients; set aside. Heat oil in uncovered wok at 400°. Add scallops; stir-fry 2 to 3 minutes until opaque. Add snow peas and tomatoes; stir-fry 1 minute. Stir cornstarch mixture; add to wok. Stir until thickened. Serve immediately.

## Kung Pao Scallops

Makes 4 servings
Preparation Time: 50 minutes; 5 minutes to cook

1 pound scallops
1 egg white, lightly beaten
1 tablespoon cornstarch
1 tablespoon dry sherry
2 tablespoons soy sauce
1½ teaspoons hot bean sauce
1½ teaspoons sugar
1½ teaspoons vinegar
1 teaspoon dry sherry
2 cups peanut oil
2 teaspoons peeled and minced fresh gingerroot
1 clove garlic, peeled and minced
4 green onions including tops, thinly sliced
10 water chestnuts, halved
20 snow peas, ends and strings removed
½ cup unsalted roasted peanuts

1 teaspoon cornstarch mixed with 3 tablespoons chicken stock or water

Mix first 4 ingredients; set aside to marinate 30 minutes. Mix next 5 ingredients; set aside. Heat oil in uncovered wok at 375°. Add scallops; stir-fry 1 minute. Remove with strainer; let drain in colander. Remove all but 1 teaspoon oil from wok. Heat oil in wok at 350°. Add next 3 ingredients; stir-fry 30 seconds. Add next 3 ingredients; stir-fry 10 seconds. Add scallops with reserved soy sauce mixture; toss to combine. Stir cornstarch mixture; add to wok; stir-fry until thickened. Serve immediately.

Kung Pao Scallops, this page

# International Dishes

## Brandied Beef

Makes 6 servings
Preparation Time: 1 hour, 45 minutes

1 teaspoon salt
1 teaspoon paprika
½ teaspoon dried basil
¼ teaspoon dried thyme
2 tablespoons flour
2 pounds beef stew meat
2 tablespoons peanut oil
1 clove garlic, peeled and crushed
1 large onion, peeled and cut in 8 wedges
½ cup beef stock
½ cup brandy
2 cups fresh mushrooms, wiped clean and halved if large
Hot cooked buttered egg noodles

Mix first 5 ingredients. Lightly dredge meat in flour mixture. Heat oil in uncovered wok at 375°. Brown meat in batches, removing to plate. Add garlic and onion; stir-fry 30 seconds. Return meat to wok with stock and brandy. Reduce heat to "simmer"; cover; simmer 1 hour. Add mushrooms; stir; cook 10 minutes, covered. Serve immediately with buttered egg noodles.

## Veal and Mushrooms

Makes 4 to 6 servings
Preparation Time: 1¼ hours

2 tablespoons peanut oil
2 pounds lean veal, cut in 1½-inch cubes
¾ pound fresh mushrooms, sliced
2 tablespoons flour
1½ cups chicken stock
Salt and freshly ground black pepper to taste
⅓ cup dry vermouth
2 tablespoons chopped fresh parsley
Hot cooked rice or noodles

Heat oil in uncovered wok at 375°. Sear veal cubes in batches; do not crowd; remove to bowl. Return veal to wok with mushrooms; stir-fry 3 minutes. Sprinkle with flour; toss to combine. Reduce heat to "simmer"; add stock and salt and pepper; mix well. Cover; simmer 50 minutes or until meat is tender. Add vermouth; toss. Sprinkle with parsley. Serve immediately on rice.

# International Dishes

## Chicken Cacciatore

Makes 6 servings
Preparation Time: 1 hour, 30 minutes

¼ **cup peanut oil**
2 **chickens, cut into serving pieces and patted dry**
2 **onions, peeled and chopped**
1 **green pepper, cored, seeded and chopped**
1 **red pepper, cored, seeded and chopped**
3 **cloves garlic, peeled and crushed**
1½ **cups tomato puree**
¼ **cup dry red wine**
1½ **teaspoons salt**
¼ **teaspoon freshly ground black pepper**
¼ **teaspoon ground allspice**
3 **tablespoons tomato paste**
1 **teaspoon dried oregano**
1 **teaspoon dried basil**
**Hot cooked spinach noodles**

Heat oil in uncovered wok at 350°. Brown chicken pieces on both sides a few at a time; place on plate. Add onions, peppers and garlic; stir-fry 2 minutes. Add remaining ingredients except chicken and noodles; bring to boil; reduce heat to "simmer" for 10 minutes. Return chicken to wok; simmer, covered, 15 to 20 minutes. Uncover; simmer 10 minutes. Serve immediately with spinach noodles.

## Greek Lamb Stew

Makes 6 servings
Preparation Time: 20 minutes; 1½ hours to cook

2 **tablespoons peanut oil**
2 **pounds boned, cubed lean lamb**
**Salt and freshly ground black pepper to taste**
3 **small onions, peeled and chopped**
2 **ribs celery, chopped**
3 **carrots, pared and thinly sliced**
2 **small cloves garlic, peeled and crushed**
2 **cups water**
4 **eggs, separated**
¼ **cup fresh lemon juice**

Heat oil in uncovered wok at 375°. Brown meat in batches; season with salt and pepper. Add onion; stir-fry until translucent. Return meat to wok with next 4 ingredients; simmer, covered, 1 hour or until meat is tender at "simmer" setting. Add more water if needed. Turn wok OFF; skim off any fat. Beat egg whites until they hold peaks; gradually beat in yolks. Slowly add lemon juice, beating constantly. Pour over stew; stir to combine and heat thoroughly. Serve immediately.

# International Dishes

## Favorite Chili

Makes 4 servings
Preparation Time: 5 minutes; 2 to 3 hours to cook

- 1 **pound coarsely ground lean beef**
- 1 **large clove garlic, peeled and crushed**
- 2 **tablespoons flour**
- 1 **teaspoon ground cumin**
- 1 to 2 **tablespoons chili powder**
- ½ **teaspoon salt**
- ¼ **teaspoon freshly ground black pepper**
- 1½ **cups vegetable cocktail juice**
- ½ **teaspoon Worcestershire sauce**
- 1 **15-ounce can red kidney beans, drained, optional**

Stir-fry meat and garlic in wok at 375° until meat is browned and crumbled. Add flour; stir to blend. Add next 6 ingredients; bring to boil. Reduce heat to "simmer"; cover; cook 2 to 3 hours, stirring occasionally. Mixture should not cook dry; add more vegetable juice if needed. Add beans 1 hour before end of cooking time, if desired. Serve immediately.

**Note:** This freezes well.

## Portuguese Codfish

Makes 4 servings
Preparation Time: 1 hour; overnight to soak fish

- 1 **pound dried codfish, soaked overnight in cold water, drained**
  **Water**
- 3 **potatoes**
- ¼ **cup peanut oil**
- 2 **large onions, peeled and sliced**
- 1 **clove garlic, peeled and crushed**
- ¼ **cup finely chopped ripe olives**
- ½ **teaspoon dried dillweed**
- ⅓ **cup dry vermouth**
  **Freshly ground black pepper to taste**
  **Fresh parsley, chopped**

Place fish in wok; cover with cold water; bring to boil at 225°; boil 20 minutes or until fish is opaque. Remove; set aside to cool; remove skin and bones if necessary. Cook potatoes in same water in wok at 225° until tender; remove; discard water. Peel and slice potatoes; set aside. Heat oil in clean wok at 350°; add onions; stir-fry until limp but not brown. Add fish, potatoes and next 5 ingredients. Gently stir-fry 3 minutes. Cover; cook at "simmer" for 10 to 15 minutes. Garnish with parsley. Serve immediately.

Favorite Chili, this page

# Desserts

## Fortune Cookies

Makes 48
Preparation Time: 15 minutes; 10 minutes to bake

**5 to 6 egg whites (¾ cup)**
**1⅔ cups sugar**
**¼ teaspoon salt**
**1 cup unsalted butter, melted**
**1 cup flour**
**¾ cup very finely chopped blanched almonds**
**½ teaspoon vanilla**
**48 fortunes written on 3 x ¾-inch strips of paper**

Preheat oven to 350°. Mix first 3 ingredients in bowl until sugar dissolves. Stir in remaining ingredients, one at a time, until well blended. Drop dough by level teaspoonfuls onto ungreased baking sheet; allow 6 cookies per sheet, spacing well apart. Bake 10 minutes or until edges are golden brown. Remove cookies, one at a time, from baking sheet. Place 1 fortune in center of each cookie; fold cookie in half; pinch sides together. Work quickly before cookies cool and harden.

## Fresh Pineapple with Grand Marnier

Makes 4 servings
Preparation Time: 15 minutes

**1 large pineapple**
**¼ cup Grand Marnier**

Cut pineapple in half lengthwise through top crown. Cut halves lengthwise, making 4 wedges. With sharp knife, cut out core that runs length of each wedge. Cut pineapple from shell in 1 piece; cut into bite-size pieces; pile back onto shell. Repeat with remaining pineapple wedges. Pour 1 tablespoon Grand Marnier over each serving; serve immediately.

**Note:** Pineapple can be cut, wrapped in plastic wrap and refrigerated 4 to 6 hours in advance; pour on Grand Marnier just before serving.

## Almond Cookies

Makes 4 dozen
Preparation Time: 15 minutes; 20 minutes to bake

| | |
|---|---|
| 1 | cup sugar |
| 1⅓ | cups shortening |
| 1 | egg |
| 1 | teaspoon almond extract |
| 3 | cups flour |
| 1 | teaspoon baking soda |
| ½ | teaspoon salt |
| 48 | blanched whole almonds |

Preheat oven to 350°. Cream sugar and shortening until fluffy. Add egg and almond extract; beat 1 minute. Sift flour, baking soda and salt together; add to creamed mixture gradually, beating constantly. Roll dough into 1-inch balls; place 1 inch apart on greased baking sheet. Press center of each ball down gently; fill depression with 1 almond. Bake 20 minutes. Remove to wire rack to cool.

**Note:** Cookies can be frozen.

## Almond Custard with Mandarin Oranges

Makes 6 to 9 servings
Preparation Time: 10 minutes; overnight to chill

| | |
|---|---|
| 2 | cups water |
| 1 | stick (about ¼ ounce) agar-agar, cut in small pieces |
| 1 | cup evaporated milk |
| ⅓ | cup sugar |
| 1 | tablespoon almond extract |
| 1 | 11-ounce can mandarin orange segments, drained |

Bring 1 cup water to boil in saucepan; add agar-agar; stir until dissolved, about 3 minutes. Add milk and sugar; return to boil. Boil 1 minute, stirring constantly. Add extract and remaining 1 cup hot water. Cook, stirring constantly, until mixture returns to boil. Strain into 9-inch square glass pan. Cool at room temperature; cover with plastic wrap; refrigerate overnight to set. To serve, cut into 1-inch cubes; divide among 6 to 9 bowls; top with orange segments. Serve immediately.

# Desserts

## Fruit Stir-Fry

Makes 4 servings
Preparation Time: 15 minutes; 10 to 15 minutes to cook

**2 firm pears (preferably Bosc), peeled, cored and cut in crosswise slices**
**3 cups semidry white wine (such as Riesling)**
**Pinch salt**
**12 strawberries, hulled and cut in crosswise slices**
**2 ripe mangoes, peeled and sectioned**
**1 kiwi fruit, peeled and sliced**
**3 tablespoons unsalted butter**
**1 pint raspberries, rinsed gently**

Combine pears, wine and salt in wok; bring just to a boil at 225°. Reduce heat to "simmer" for 2 to 3 minutes or until pears are just tender. Add strawberries; simmer 1 minute. Add mangoes; simmer 1 minute. Add kiwi fruit; simmer 1 minute. Fruit should be tender, but not falling apart. Carefully remove fruit with strainer; keep warm. Boil liquid in wok at 400° to reduce by one-half. Lower heat to 250°; swirl in butter. Return cooked fruit to sauce. Add raspberries; mix gently just until raspberries are warmed through. Remove fruit to individual bowls using strainer; boil sauce further if it seems too thin. Spoon sauce over fruit.

**Note:** This makes a luscious sauce for vanilla ice cream.

## Hong Kong Sundae

Makes enough sauce for 6 to 8 servings
Preparation Time: 10 minutes; 3 to 4 hours to chill

**1 8½-ounce can crushed pineapple with juice**
**2 tablespoons cornstarch**
**1 11-ounce can mandarin orange segments with liquid**
**6 to 8 preserved kumquats, drained and chopped**
**2 tablespoons chopped preserved ginger**
**Vanilla ice cream**

Mix 2 tablespoons of the pineapple juice with cornstarch; set aside. Place pineapple and remaining juice, orange segments and liquid, kumquats and ginger in top of double boiler over medium heat. Heat to just below boiling. Stir cornstarch mixture; add to double boiler. Stir until thickened. Pour into bowl; refrigerate until completely cold. Serve as sauce over ice cream.

Clockwise, from top: Almond Cookies, page 89
Fruit Stir-Fry, this page; Melon Balls in Liqueur, page 92

# Desserts

## Melon Balls in Liqueur

Makes 3 servings
Preparation Time: 30 minutes plus chilling time

½ cup watermelon balls, seeds removed
½ cup honeydew melon balls
½ cup cantaloupe melon balls
3 tablespoons melon-flavored liqueur

Mix melon balls gently in glass bowl; chill thoroughly. To serve, divide melon balls equally among 3 glass serving bowls; drizzle 1 tablespoon liqueur over each bowl. Serve immediately.

## Custard with Oriental Sauce

Makes 6 servings
Preparation Time: 10 minutes; 30 to 40 minutes to bake; 3 to 4 hours to chill

3 eggs
3 tablespoons sugar
⅛ teaspoon salt
¼ teaspoon almond extract
½ teaspoon vanilla extract
2¼ cups scalded milk
Oriental Fruit

Preheat oven to 350°. Beat eggs, sugar, salt, almond and vanilla extracts together in bowl. Gradually add milk, stirring constantly. Divide equally among 6 custard cups. Place cups in large shallow pan; fill pan with boiling water that reaches to level of custard in cups. Bake 30 to 40 minutes or until knife inserted in center of custard comes out clean. Cool at room temperature 10 minutes; cover; chill thoroughly. Prepare Oriental Fruit. To serve, run knife around outside edges of custards; invert onto serving dishes; top with Oriental Fruit.

### Oriental Fruit

⅓ cup sugar
1 tablespoon cornstarch
1 cup fresh orange juice
1 11-ounce can mandarin orange segments, drained
1 11-ounce can litchi nuts, drained

Stir sugar and cornstarch together in 2-quart saucepan. Place over low heat; gradually add orange juice, stirring constantly. Bring to boil, stirring constantly until thickened. Remove from heat; stir in orange segments and nuts. Cover and chill.

# Glossary

**Bamboo Shoots** Young shoots of tropical bamboo. Sold whole or sliced in cans. After opening, rinse in cold water. Store in water in refrigerator up to 1 week. Change water every 2 days.

**Bean Curd** Also known as tofu. A nutritious, low-calorie source of protein. Made of pressed pureed soybeans formed into cakes. It is white and has the consistency of firm custard. Bland in taste, it absorbs the flavor of other ingredients. Can be fried, simmered, baked, steamed, or used in stir-frying. Store in water in refrigerator up to 1 week. Change water daily.

**Bean Sauce\*** Made of soybeans, flour, salt and water. Hot bean sauce is a more spicy version used in Szechwan dishes. After opening, refrigerate in tightly covered jar. Keeps indefinitely.

**Bean Sprouts** Tiny sprouts that are white, sweet, plump and crunchy. Fresh sprouts are preferable to canned sprouts. Rinse in cold water before using. Store in water in refrigerator up to 1 week. Change water daily.

**Black Beans\*** Salted and fermented, these beans season fish and meat dishes. Store in tightly covered container indefinitely.

**Bok Choy** Green vegetable with long white stalks and ruffled leaves. Store in plastic wrap in refrigerator up to 1 week.

**Cellophane Noodles\*** Also known as bean thread or vermicelli. Made of mung bean flour and look as if they are made from cellophane. Must be presoaked if used in soups; not necessary to presoak for deep-frying. Keep indefinitely.

**Chicken Stock** Interchangeable with canned chicken broth although homemade chicken stock is preferable.

**Dried Orange or Tangerine Peel\*** Used for flavoring meat and poultry. Keeps indefinitely.

**Dried Red Pepper Flakes\*** Made from dried orange or red hot peppers. Include seeds which are essential for hotness. Keep indefinitely.

**Ears of Baby Corn** Tiny ears of corn, 2 to 3 inches long, sold in cans. Store in liquid in covered can in refrigerator up to 6 days.

**Egg Roll Skins** Squares of egg noodle dough in which to place filling. Store in refrigerator up to 5 days. May be frozen.

**Five-Spice Powder\*** Combination of 5 ground spices — cinnamon, fennel, star anise, cloves and Szechwan peppercorns. Used for stewing and barbecuing meats. Reddish brown in color. Keeps indefinitely.

**Garlic** Do not substitute garlic powder. Never burn garlic while cooking, or it will impart bitter taste. Store in dry place.

**Ginger, preserved\*** Used in sweet and sour dishes for color and flavoring. Store in tightly covered jar in refrigerator. Keeps indefinitely.

**Gingerroot, fresh** Very important seasoning in stir-fry cooking. There is no substitute. Sold by the piece or by weight, fresh gingerroot is knobby in appearance. Always peel before using. Wrap in plastic; keep at room temperature 2 to 3 weeks. Never refrigerate. Can be peeled, sliced and frozen; do not thaw before using.

**Green Onion** Also called scallion. Long, thin onion with white and green part.

**Hoisin Sauce\*** Spicy reddish-brown sauce with creamy consistency, made of Chinese pumpkin, sugar, spices and soy sauce. After opening, store in covered jar several weeks.

# Glossary

**Litchi*** Subtropical fruit. Delicious in sweet and sour sauce. Used in desserts. Store in tightly covered jar in refrigerator several days.

**Mushrooms, Chinese Dried Black*** Rinse and soak in hot water 20 minutes before using. Use caps, discard tough stems. Keep indefinitely.

**Mushrooms, Cloud Ear*** Also known as tree ears or fungus mushrooms. Black and crinkled, they expand two to three times their dried size when soaked. Soft in texture, subtle in taste. Must be soaked in hot water before using. Cook with vegetables, chicken, meat or soup. Keep indefinitely.

**Mushrooms, Straw*** Delicious with crab meat. After opening, refrigerate, covered with water, in jar. Change water every 2 days. Keep several weeks.

**Mustard, Chinese** Used for dipping sauce. Make in small amounts; mix powdered or dry mustard with cold water and allow to mellow 30 minutes to remove harsh, bitter taste. Hot and pungent. Keeps indefinitely.

**Oyster Sauce*** Thick Cantonese sauce made from oyster extract, but has no fishy taste or odor. Adds flavor to meat, poultry and noodles. Store covered in refrigerator several months.

**Peanut Oil** Preferred for stir-frying. Can be reused if strained and refrigerated. Discard when dark and full of residue. Oil for cooking fish should be kept separate and reused only for fish. Refrigerate after use.

**Plum Sauce*** Made of plums, ginger, apricots, chilies, vinegar, sugar and water. Used as condiment. Store in covered container in refrigerator a few months.

**Rice, glutinous*** Also known as sweet rice. Round grains that become soft and sticky when cooked. Used for making dumplings, sweet dishes and poultry stuffing. Keeps indefinitely.

**Rice Sticks** Also called rice noodles. White, thin, fragile and slightly wavy, these sticks are made from ground rice. Used deep-fried and in soups. Store on shelf indefinitely.

**Sesame Seed Oil*** Reddish brown, made from roasted sesame seed. Generally used as seasoning; the thicker the oil, the better the flavor. Keeps indefinitely.

**Snow Peas** Also known as pea pods. Flat, light green, crisp and sweet. Always select thin snow peas. Avoid frozen pea pods because they give up too much moisture in stir-fried dishes. Remove ends and strings. Slice through stem end, but do not sever string. Pull stem end and attached string down pod. Repeat on opposite end for other string. Usually left whole for cooking and eating. Store in refrigerator 1 to 3 days.

**Soy Sauce** One of the most important seasonings in stir-fry cookery. There are two kinds. Thin soy sauce has a clear brown color and a beanlike aroma. Use it for delicate dishes. Dark soy sauce is very dark in color, has a sheen and is slightly thicker than light soy sauce. Dark soy sauce is slightly sweet and the bean aroma is muted. Store on shelf indefinitely.

**Star Anise*** Reddish-brown Chinese spice resembling 8-pointed star. Smells like licorice. Flavors meat and poultry. Store in covered jar indefinitely.

**Tofu** See bean curd.

**Water Chestnuts** Used as vegetable with meat and poultry. Delicious with snow peas. Sold whole or sliced in cans. After opening, cover with water and refrigerate. Change water twice a week. Keeps several weeks.

**Wine, Chinese** Rice wine fortified to the strength of sherry. Use dry sherry as substitute, but never cooking sherry.

**Won Ton Skins** Small squares or rounds of egg noodle dough in which fillings are placed. Sold in 1-pound packages. Keep refrigerated 1 week. Can be frozen.

*denotes items found in Oriental and/or specialty food stores

# Index

# Index